Faith-Building Meetings for Upper-Elementary Kids

Compiled by Group Books

Loveland, Colorado

Faith-Building Meetings for Upper-Elementary Kids
Copyright © 1991 by Group Books

Third Printing, 1994

Credits
Edited by Michael D. Warden and Stephen Parolini
Cover and book designed by Jill Christopher

Scripture quotations from The Everyday Bible, New Century Version, copyright © 1987, 1988 by Word Publishing, Dallas, TX 75039. Used by permission.

Library of Congress Cataloging-in-Publication Data
Faith-building meetings for upper-elementary kids / compiled by Group Books ; [edited by Michael D. Warden and Stephen Parolini].
     p.   cm.
     ISBN 1-55945-054-1 :
     1. Children—Religious life. 2. Children—Conduct of life. I. Warden, Michael
D. II. Parolini, Stephen, 1959-   . III. Group Books (Firm)
BV4571.2.F33   1991   90-23714
                                                                                        CIP

268'.432—dc20
Printed in the United States of America

Contents

PART 3: **MY FRIENDS**

PART 4: **MY WORLD**

Introduction

Attention!
This is a test. Name five topics you think elementary-age kids would include in a list of their 20 most important issues.

1.
2.
3.
4.
5.

What did you write? Video games? New clothes? How about skateboarding? If you wrote any answers like these, think again! According to recent surveys of upper-elementary-age children, their top concerns include:

- Divorce;
- Death;
- Drug and alcohol abuse;
- Sex; and
- Making friends.

Whew! Not exactly what the Cleavers would've talked about over dinner, is it?

Kids are growing up faster than ever. It would've been strange indeed to hear "the Beaver" talk to his father about the pressure to take crack. But elementary kids in many cities today talk about drugs every day. And a frightening number of those kids do more than just talk about it.

Kids need opportunities to ask questions about important topics. And they need to hear the answers God provides for them through his Word.

That's why we've compiled *Faith-Building Meetings for Upper-Elementary Kids*. The 20 lively meetings in this volume hit on topics kids care about and need to understand. The simple-to-follow outlines combine fun with fast-paced action. And the timely discussions and Bible studies bring God's truth to where kids live—in a fast-paced world that's trying to make them grow up too soon, a world that's confronting them with temptations most adults didn't encounter until their late teen-age years.

Use these meetings to fit your group's needs. If you're just beginning an elementary group, take your own survey and discover top interests. A survey could be as simple as listing all the topics covered in this book, then asking kids to choose the ones that interest them most. Leave space for kids to add their own ideas for activities they'd like.

The meetings in *Faith-Building Meetings for Upper-Elementary Kids* are divided into four sections:

● **Introduction**—This section gives an overview and focuses on the topic.

● **Objectives**—Each meeting lists several objectives that highlight facts kids will learn or activities they'll participate in.

● **The Meeting**—This section contains step-by-step ideas and easy-to-follow instructions. Meetings each start with an opening activity to get kids acquainted with the topic. Meetings each close with a prayer, snack or other activity that wraps up and reinforces the lesson.

● **Handouts**—All necessary handouts are included. You have permission to photocopy them for local church use.

Whether you use the meetings in this book for weekly get-togethers, retreats or lock-ins, use them to meet your kids' needs. And have fun!

Part 1
My Faith

What's God Like?

"**Y**ou can't know what something is like unless you see it!"

Many times people think that's true—especially when we talk about God. After all, how can we understand who "God" is unless we see him firsthand?

Our understanding of God doesn't come through sight but through a variety of experiences that reveal him. For example, we can read books, listen to others or notice what God is doing in the lives of people around us. In all of these ways, we can learn more about God. In this meeting, help kids learn about God through several enlightening experiences.

Objectives

In this meeting, elementary kids will:
- experience what it's like to learn about something;
- discover ways to learn about God;
- learn why it's good to know about God; and
- understand the difference between knowing God and knowing about God.

The Meeting

1 Person, place or thing

(Photocopy and cut apart the "What Am I?" slips on page 14.)

Form teams of four to six by having kids form a line. Then "number" them off using different adjectives, such as "young," "sour" or "happy." Use as many adjectives as you need.

Hold up the "What Am I?" slips and say: **We're going to play a guessing game. Each team will win points by being the first**

by
Janet Kageler

to guess the name of the person, place or thing the clues describe.

One at a time, have volunteers choose a "What Am I?" slip. Tell volunteers not to let others see what's written on their slips.

Next, have volunteers each create clues to describe their item. For example, if a slip has "George Washington" on it, a volunteer might give the following clues: "I'm a person," "I lived a long time ago" and "I was an American President."

Award 100 points to the team that guesses the answer first. In case of a tie, award 100 points to each team that answers correctly.

After all the slips have been played, give the winning team a rousing round of applause. Then call everyone together and ask:

● **Was this game easy? Why or why not?**
● **How'd you figure out what was written on the slips?**

Say: **We know about all of the people, places or things on the slips, but we've probably never seen them. God is like that too. We learn about him and can get to know him even though we've never seen him in person.**

2 Illustrating words

(Create a list of simple nouns kids can easily illustrate; for example, "bird" or "apple." Include at least six words on your list. For each team of four to six, you'll need a note pad and a pencil. For each person, you'll need a sheet of paper and a pencil.)

Have kids stay in their teams.

Before starting this game, have teams each give a cheer. Award 100 points for the noisiest cheer.

Have teams each select one person to represent their team. Give representatives each a note pad and a pencil. Show all the representatives one word from your list. On "go," have the representatives each draw a picture of the word for their team. Don't allow representatives to speak or use any letters or numbers in their drawings. The first team to guess the correct answer gets 100 points.

Repeat the process until kids each have had at least one chance to draw a picture for their team. Award each of the winning team members with a friendly back rub.

Call everyone together and give kids each a sheet of paper and a pencil. Say: **Now that we've drawn items we're all fa-**

miliar with, let's try something a little more challenging. On your paper, draw a picture of God.

Encourage kids to use their imaginations and think about what God might look like. When everyone is finished, have kids each explain their pictures. Congratulate kids on their creativity and say: **Everyone has an idea about what God is like, but he's much harder to draw than an apple or a bird. And no one knows exactly what he looks like since we can't see him. But there are several ways we can learn about who God is.**

3 Ways to know

(You'll need tape, newsprint and a marker.)

Have kids form a circle. Tape a sheet of newsprint to the wall. Ask:

● **What are some ways we learn about God?**

List kids' responses on newsprint. Then say: **There are a few important ways people learn about God. They can:**

● **Read**—The Bible or other good books about God can teach us a lot about what God is like.

● **Listen**—Others who know about God, such as Sunday school teachers or pastors, can help us understand God much better when we listen to them. We can also listen to Christian music that describes God.

● **Pray**—We learn more about God when we see how he listens to us and answers our prayers.

● **Look around**—God's work is all around us—in nature and in other people. We can learn a lot about God just by watching the people and places around us.

4 Dig into God's Word

(For each group of four, you'll need a Bible.)

Have kids stay in their groups. Say: **Let's discover more about what God is like by looking in the Bible—God's Word.**

Give groups each a Bible and assign them each one of these scripture passages:

● Psalm 90:1-2 (God will live forever.)
● Psalm 139:1-2 (God knows everything about me.)

● Psalm 139:7-8 (God is everywhere.)

● 1 John 4:16 (God is love.)

Help groups find their passages in the Bible if necessary. Use an easy-to-understand version such as *The Everyday Bible* (Word) or *The Living Bible* (Tyndale). Have groups each read their passage and decide what the passage says about God. Give hints if groups have trouble deciding which of God's attributes is described.

Then have groups each create a human sculpture to describe their attribute of God. For example, a group illustrating "God is love" might arrange themselves on the floor in a heart shape. Have groups each display their sculpture, and have other groups try to guess the attribute of God they're describing.

Applaud each group's efforts. Then ask:

● **What does it mean that God will live forever?**

● **What does it mean that God knows everything? is present everywhere?**

● **What does it mean that God is love?**

● **Why can we be glad God is like this?**

Say: **We can be glad God has these qualities because they help us know God loves us and is strong enough to take care of all our needs. Let's celebrate God's wonderful qualities by enjoying a snack together.**

5 Discovery snacks

(For each person, you'll need a choice of two snacks. Make sure each snack is easy to describe, using only adjectives. For each person, you'll also need a glass of water.)

Before serving the snack, give kids a choice. Describe the two snacks, but don't tell kids what the snacks are. For example, one snack could be "cold, smooth, white and sweet" (vanilla ice cream). Another snack could be "gooey, brown and cakelike" (brownie). Have kids guess what the snacks are, then give kids each the snack of their choice along with a glass of water.

After the snack, say: **Just as you could identify the snacks by my description, so you can learn to recognize God by understanding what he's like. But real joy comes in knowing him, not just knowing about him. That's like the difference between identifying the snack and tasting it. Let's pray together that God will help us get to know him better as we learn more about him.**

6 I wanna know God

(No supplies needed.)

Form a circle and hold hands. Have kids each offer this sentence prayer: "Dear Lord, help me know you better as I learn about you." Close by thanking God for his qualities and asking God to help kids to know him better.

"What Am I?"

Instructions: Photocopy and cut apart these slips to use in activity 1.

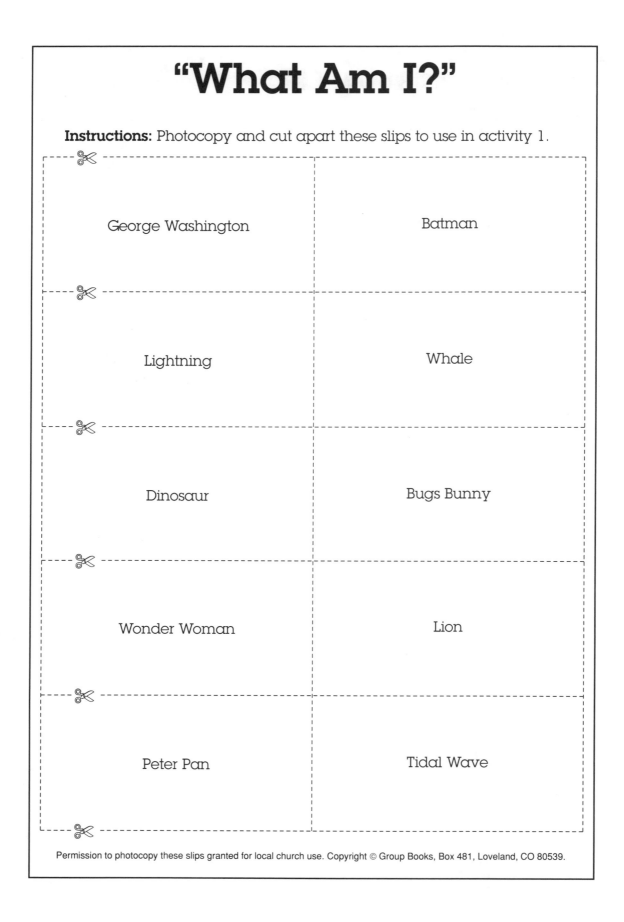

George Washington

Batman

Lightning

Whale

Dinosaur

Bugs Bunny

Wonder Woman

Lion

Peter Pan

Tidal Wave

More Like Jesus

It's easy to say Jesus is part of our lives. It's much harder to live that way. Elementary kids can begin to examine what it really means to be a Christian and evaluate how well they live out their faith.

In this meeting kids will see how Jesus fits in their lives. They'll search the scriptures for Christlike qualities and discover how they can be more like Jesus every day.

Objectives

In this meeting, elementary kids will:
- explore qualities of a Christian;
- role play Jesus' parables;
- build a "Christian" with Christlike characteristics; and
- choose Christlike qualities to build into their lives.

The Meeting

1 The perfect fit

(For each person, photocopy and cut apart the "Cross Puzzle" handout on page 19. Place each complete set of puzzle pieces in a separate paper bag.)

Hand each child a bag with the five pieces of the "Cross Puzzle" inside. Say: **When we lay out all the pieces of our lives, we realize they just don't fit together without Jesus in the middle. He needs to teach us how to be like him.**

Give kids one minute to solve the puzzle and form a cross with their pieces. Don't allow kids to look at each other's progress or help each other. When the time is up, collect the puzzle pieces, commend kids' efforts and move on to the next activity.

by
Linda Snyder

2 Christ code

(For each person, you'll need a "Christ Code" handout on page 20 and a pencil.)

Say: **In the Bible passage I'm going to give you, Jesus tells us the part he wants to play in our lives.**

Form groups of no more than four. Distribute the "Christ Code" handout and a pencil to each person. Have group members work together to decode and unscramble the message as quickly as possible. When a group has completed the handout, have its members stand up and shout. Award the winning group a big "hooray!"

Have the winning group read aloud the verse from the "Christ Code" handout. Then ask:

● **Was it easy to complete the puzzle or decode the scripture? Why or why not?**

● **Is it easy to act like Jesus? Why or why not?**

● **How can we act more like Jesus?**

Say: **People who are having a good time might say, "This is the life!" But Jesus says we find real life only when we obey him. He can make our lives good as we try to act more like him each day.**

3 People blueprints

(You'll need newsprint, tape and a marker. For each group of four, you'll need a "Body Parts" handout on page 21 and a pencil.)

Have kids get back into their groups. Give each group a "Body Parts" handout and a pencil. Have groups each brainstorm ideas for using their body parts for God; for example: eyes to see people in need, ears to listen, mouths to share God's Word or arms to hug.

When groups are finished, tape a sheet of newsprint to the wall. Then ask:

● **What actions did your group come up with?**

Write kids' responses on the newsprint. Then say: **You've mentioned several good ways we can use our bodies for God. Let's look at other ways we can be more like Jesus.**

4 Parable plays

(You'll need four Bibles, newsprint, tape and a marker.)

Form four groups. Give groups each a Bible. Assign groups each one of the following parables to silently act out:

- Matthew 18:23-24 (parable of the unmerciful servant)
- Luke 6:46-49 (parable of the wise and foolish builders)
- Luke 10:25-37 (parable of the good Samaritan)
- Luke 18:9-14 (parable of the Pharisee and tax collector)

Give groups each five minutes to prepare a pantomime of the scripture. Have adult volunteers work with groups to help them design the pantomimes. Give creative suggestions and keep kids organized so they can work together.

When groups are ready, have them each pantomime their parable for the whole group as you or another adult reads aloud the scripture. Applaud each group's performance.

After the parable pantomimes, tape a sheet of newsprint to the wall. Brainstorm with kids how the people in the stories acted like Jesus. Write kids' ideas on the newsprint.

Say: **There's one list of personality traits in the Bible that tells us what it means to be like Jesus. I'll read it to you, then we'll add the attitudes to our list.**

Read aloud Galatians 5:22-23. Add the fruits of the Spirit to your newsprint list.

5 Build a Christian

(For each group of four, you'll need tape, magazines, markers, yarn, aluminum foil, pipe cleaners, construction paper and scissors.)

Have kids stay in their groups. Give groups each their Christian-building craft supplies. Choose one person from each group to be the "model." Have groups each create a Christian by decorating the model with symbols of traits and characteristics kids think a Christian should have. Have groups use the newsprint list you've made for ideas. They can tape magazine words and pictures to the model, or tape words and symbols they've written on paper. Have groups create body parts and label them with Christian traits. For example, they might cut out a construction paper heart and label it "love."

Emphasize creativity, and give groups time to do a thorough

job. When all the groups have finished, have them each present their "Christian" to the whole group. Be sure they each explain their decorations completely. Ask:

- **What was fun about creating your Christian?**
- **What was hard about creating your Christian?**

Read aloud several qualities kids listed on their models. Ask:

- **How can we live out these qualities?**
- **Why should we try to act like Jesus in all we do?**

◁6 Food for thought

(For each person, you'll need a fruit-flavor Life Savers candy.)

Have group members each pick one Christlike trait from their model they'd like to have; for example a heart to love or ears to listen. Encourage kids to each take their trait home and tape it near their bed as a reminder to be more like Jesus.

Distribute fruit-flavor Life Savers candies and close with this prayer: **Dear God, thank you for sending Jesus to be a part of our lives. Help us to work on being more like Jesus. Give us the strength to really be a "Life Saver" for others. In Jesus' name, amen.**

Cross Puzzle

Instructions: Photocopy and cut apart enough of these puzzles so each child can have one. Place each complete set of pieces in a separate paper bag.

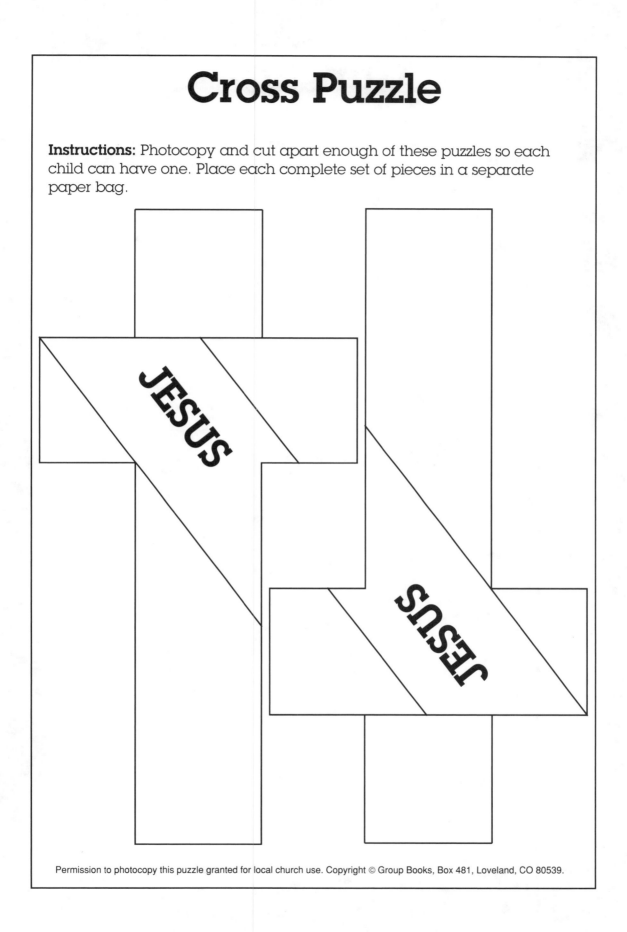

Christ Code

Instructions: Use the guide below to decode the letters in the verse at the bottom of the page.

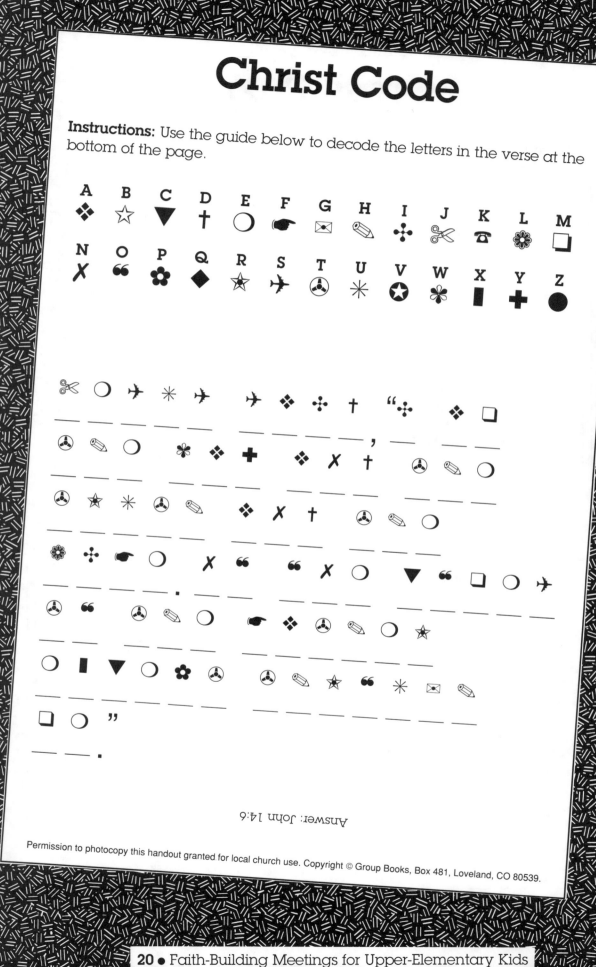

Answer: John 14:6

BODY PARTS

Instructions: For each body part below, name a way you can use that body part for God; for example, eyes to see people in need or ears to listen.

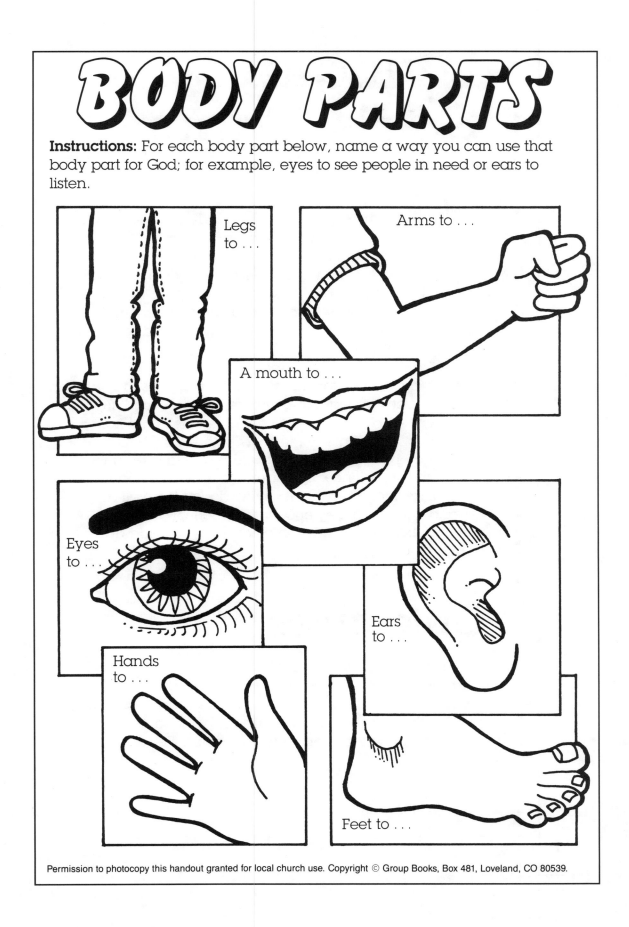

Legs to . . .

Arms to . . .

A mouth to . . .

Eyes to . . .

Ears to . . .

Hands to . . .

Feet to . . .

Living in God's Armor

Truth, justice and freedom!
That's the cry of the Superfriends—a top-notch band of superheroes including Superman, Wonder Woman and Flash—who take lodging in the world-renowned Hall of Justice somewhere in America. For several years, each Saturday morning, the Superfriends would fly, run, press and punch their way across kids' TV screens, beating the enemy and cornering the criminal. And the bad guy would inevitably end up in the slammer.

Right always won over wrong.

But it's not so easy for kids in real life. Cartoons may draw a clear line between right and wrong, but real-world choices aren't that simple. Kids need to be able to tell right from wrong, or good from best, in order to grow in their faith.

Fortunately, the Bible tells how kids can face an uncertain world with confidence. By learning about and wearing God's spiritual armor, kids can effectively dodge the well-disguised lies and half-truths they encounter at school and home. And they can become mighty "little heroes" who stand up for God's truth and justice.

Objectives

In this meeting elementary kids will:
- make armor that describes who they are;
- learn about Jesus' armor for Christian warriors;
- decide "right vs. wrong" using the armor of God; and
- choose how they can wear the armor of God.

by
Linda Snyder

The Meeting

1 My armor

(For each person, you'll need a marker and a paper-bag vest. Refer to the illustration below to see how to prepare the vests.)

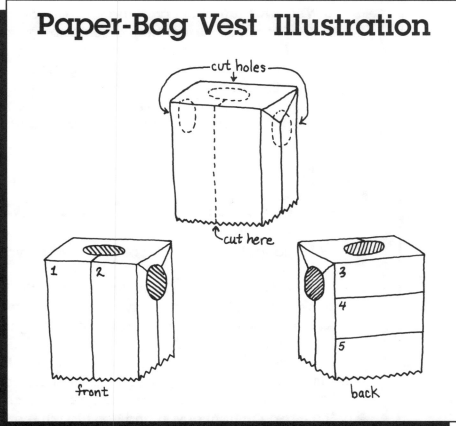

Paper-Bag Vest Illustration

cut holes

cut here

front

back

Give kids each a paper-bag vest. Say: **We're taking an imaginary trip back in time, the time of King Arthur and the Knights of the Round Table. People who lived then had armor to protect them and to identify which kingdom they belonged to. Today, we're going to make armor that shows who we are and which kingdom we belong to.**

Give kids each a marker. Have kids each draw lines to divide their coat into five sections—left-front, right-front, top-back, middle-back, and bottom-back (see the illustration above). Then have kids each draw pictures or symbols in each of their five sections according to these categories:

1. My favorite subject in school;
2. What I like to do best;
3. My favorite Bible story;
4. Something I believe is wrong; and
5. Something I believe is right.

When everyone is finished, form teams of five or fewer. If possible, include an adult on each team. Have kids each don their armor. Then have team members explain their armor to each other.

Call everyone together and ask:

- **What was fun about creating your armor?**
- **How does your armor help others know who you are?**

Say: **Wearing your armor is fun because it helps you show others who you are. Jesus has an armor he gives us to wear too. And like your armor, it identifies us as his children. Let's play a game that shows what it's like to live without Jesus' armor on. Then we'll take a look at what Jesus' armor is like.**

2 Around the round table

(You'll need a stopwatch or a watch with a second hand. For each team of five or fewer, you'll need a 12-foot string.)

Have kids remove their armor and stay in their teams. Give teams each a 12-foot string. Have teams each use their string to create a circle on the floor. Designate a starting point on each circle. Beginning at the starting point and following the outside of the circle, have team members each line up "train style"— with their hands on the waist of the person in front of them.

Say: **On "go," run around your circle five times. Don't let go of the person in front of you and don't touch the string, or you'll have to start over. The first team to successfully run around the circle five times wins.**

Have teams race one at a time. Use a stopwatch or a watch with a second hand to time the races. If you have time after the first race is finished, try these fun variations:

- Jump with both feet three times around the circle.
- Walk backwards three times around the circle.
- Skip four times around the circle.
- Hop on one foot two times around the circle.

After all the races are finished, announce the overall winner. Have all the other teams surround the winning team and give "high fives." Ask:

● How do you feel after running around in circles?

● What was hard about this game?

Say: **Without Jesus' armor to protect us, we can easily get "dizzy" and confused about what's right and wrong. And no matter how much we try to get out of a bad situation, we can end up right where we started, just like we did in this race.**

3 Action armor

(You'll need a Bible. For each team of five or fewer, you'll need to make an "armor bag" by filling paper bags each with paper, aluminum foil, cardboard for shields and swords, markers, crayons, glue, tape and scissors.)

Read aloud Ephesians 6:10-18. Say: **Just as your vest of armor describes who you are, so each piece of Jesus' armor tells us something about him. And he gives us his armor so we can be like him.**

Give an "armor bag" to each team. Using the armor-bag materials, have teams each construct and label the items below as you describe them:

● Belt of truth (Jesus never lies);

● Breastplate of righteousness (Jesus always does what's right);

● "Gospel of peace" shoes (Jesus gives us peace);

● Shield of faith (Jesus trusts God);

● Helmet of salvation (Jesus saves us from sin); and

● Sword of the Spirit (Jesus is the living Word of God).

It's okay if some kids don't understand the connection between the armor and Jesus' character. They'll remember the experience and perhaps come to understanding later.

Have each team dress one person in the armor. Then gather everyone together and have teams each present their armor. Have kids vote on which armor is the silliest or the best-looking. Then ask:

● **What was fun about making the armor? Explain.**

● **Why should we wear Jesus' armor?**

Say: **Jesus' armor protects us from doing what's wrong. Just as you placed your armor on your team member, so you need to place Jesus' armor on yourself each day. That means believing Jesus protects you and helps you choose what's right.**

4 | Super-soldier situations

(For each team of five or fewer, you'll need a situation from the "Soldier Situations" handout on page 27.)

Have kids stay in their teams. Say: **Wearing Jesus' armor helps us make decisions about what's right or wrong. I'll give each team a situation. You decide what Jesus would do if he were faced with that situation. The armor-clad "soldiers" in each team will act out the responses.**

Give teams each a different situation from the "Soldier Situations" handout. It's okay if more than one team has the same situation. Give teams time to read their situations, decide what to do and prepare skits. When everyone is ready, have teams each present their skit. Applaud each team's efforts. Then ask:

● **Is it always easy to do what's right? Why or why not?**
● **How can Jesus help you do what's right?**

Say: **Jesus gives us his armor so we can be strong and wise like he is. Although we can't see Jesus' armor, it's with us and can help us make good decisions about right and wrong.**

5 | What-will-you-wear worship

(For each person, you'll need a piece of aluminum foil.)

Have kids form a circle. Give each child a piece of aluminum foil. Have kids each sculpt a piece of Jesus' armor they want to wear; for example, a shield of faith or a sword of the Spirit.

When everyone is finished, have kids each don their armor and explain why they chose it. Have kids form a circle and raise their arms in a salute toward the center of the circle. Close with a simple dedication prayer thanking God for the armor that helps kids choose what's right.

Soldier Situations

Instructions: Photocopy and cut apart these situations to use in activity 4.

✂ -

TESSIE'S TEST

It's Wednesday night and Tessie's favorite TV show is coming on. Her parents have gone to a meeting and she's promised to study while they're gone. If she watches the TV show, she'll have to cram for her test. And she probably won't get an A if she crams. Her parents will never know, and a B won't hurt her final grade. What should she do?

✂ -

FRED'S FRIEND

Fred's mom doesn't like his best friend. She told Fred he can't see his friend anymore. Fred knows he can see still his friend. He can just tell his mom he's going to someone else's house. Then he can go see his friend and be back in time for dinner. What should he do?

✂ -

GREG'S GOD

The guys Greg hangs around with never go to church. They think church is for nerds. Every week they ask Greg to play ball with them on Sunday morning. Most of the time Greg makes up excuses. Now he's wondering whether he should tell them he goes to church and see if they'll change their game time so he can play. He's worried they'll laugh at him. What should he do?

✂ -

FRANNY'S FIGHT

Franny's best friend went to a party with a guy Franny likes. At school everyone's talking about the "new couple." Franny is mad and feels betrayed. When Franny sees her friend, she feels so angry she thinks about punching her out or calling her a few "good" names. What should she do?

✂ -

Part 2
My Self

Hey! Look at Me!

We live in a superficial world.
People are sometimes judged by whether their belts match their shoes, or whether their hairstyles are current. Especially in the United States, we've learned the importance of making our outside look good so people will accept our inside.

Unfortunately, kids aren't immune to these superficial rules. Even early in elementary life, kids are ridiculed for being too fat or too thin, or for wearing outdated clothing styles. Kids want to be accepted, but they can hit a wall of rejection if they appear to be less than "cool."

To fight the pressures kids face, they need to see themselves as valuable. A clean and neat appearance is important, but kids need to see their real value in what God sees "inside."

Objectives

In this meeting, elementary kids will:
- discuss what they like and don't like about their bodies;
- explore the importance of clothing styles;
- learn why they shouldn't judge people by the way they look; and
- understand that God sees them each as uniquely beautiful.

The Meeting

1 My best feature is . . .

(For each person, you'll need a "Feature Me" handout on page 35 and a pencil.)

Give kids each a "Feature Me" handout and a pencil. Say:
Have a different person sign each blank on your handout

by
Janel Kauffman

according to which body part he or she thinks is your best feature. Let kids laugh and have fun with the activity.

When everyone is finished, ask:

● **Do you like every part of your body? Why or why not?**
● **Which parts do you like? Explain.**
● **Which parts don't you like? Explain.**
● **How do you feel about the parts you don't like?**

Say: **Today we're going to talk about the way we look. We're going to discuss things about ourselves we like and don't like, and compare our outlook with God's outlook on our appearance. Let's start our "look at looks" by having fun with some "stylish" clothes.**

2 "Hi gorgeous" relay

(Fill two suitcases each with these items: hat, shirt, pants, gloves, jacket, tie, scarf, boots, socks, wig and mirror.)

Open the two suitcases filled with clothes. Form two teams and have them each line up behind a starting line about 10 feet away from the suitcases. Assign a suitcase to each team. On "go," have team members run to the suitcase one at a time, put on all the clothes, look in the mirror, yell "Hi gorgeous," take off the clothes, run back to the team, and tag the next person to repeat the process. The first team to have everyone complete the process wins.

Award the winning team with a "hip, hip, hooray!" Then ask:

● **Why was it fun to dress up in these clothes?**
● **Is what you wear important to you? Why or why not?**
● **Do you notice what other people wear? Why or why not?**

Say: **It's important to be neat and clean, but what people wear doesn't always say what kind of people they are. We need to look under the surface.**

3 Taste-test time

(Prepare five bowls of vanilla pudding. Mix a different food coloring into four of the bowls; for example, red, green, blue and yellow. Leave one bowl uncolored. Number the bowls 1 to 5. For each person, you'll need a 3×5 card, a pencil and a plastic spoon.)

Set out the five bowls of pudding. Give kids each a 3×5 card, a pencil and a plastic spoon. Have kids each number their card 1 to 5. First, have kids try to guess the pudding flavors without tasting them. Usually kids will guess a flavor that corresponds with its color. Then have kids each taste the puddings and write the flavor of each pudding next to the appropriate number.

When kids are finished, have some tell what they wrote. Then give the correct answer. Kids will be surprised that all of the bowls of pudding are vanilla. Ask:

● **What surprised you about our taste test?**

● **Why was it easier to identify the flavors after you tasted them?**

● **What made you think the pudding flavors were different?**

● **How is judging the pudding by its looks like how we sometimes judge people?**

Read aloud 1 Samuel 16:7. Say: **The outward appearance of someone doesn't always tell what's on the inside. We should look beyond how people look to learn what they're really like.**

Mirror, mirror, on the wall

(You'll need a Bible and a large mirror. For each person, you'll need a sheet of paper and a pencil.)

Give kids each paper and a pencil. Have kids each draw what they'd like to look like or list qualities they wish they had. When kids are finished, have some kids explain what they drew or tell what they wrote.

Say: **All of us have ways we can improve our appearance. Eating right, getting exercise and being neat and clean help us feel good about ourselves. But there are also unchangeable qualities in each of us. How we look isn't totally within our control. But it's important to understand that we're each uniquely beautiful to God. Each of us is special.**

Read aloud Psalm 139:14. Set out a large mirror. Have kids each look in the mirror. As each person looks in the mirror, have the rest of the group say aloud, "God thinks you're beautiful (or handsome)."

Some kids in your group may find this activity embarrassing or uncomfortable. Be sensitive to kids' feelings, but encourage everyone to participate. It's important that all kids feel they're special and worthy of special attention.

5 It's cookie time

(For each person, you'll need a large sugar cookie or a gingerbread man. You'll also need a variety of icings, candies and raisins.)

Set out large sugar cookies or gingerbread men and a variety of icings, candies and raisins. Have kids each decorate their cookies to look like themselves. When everyone is finished, have kids display their cookie look-alikes.

Say: **Even though you may come close to copying the way you look, no one can ever copy the unique qualities that make you special to God and to others.**

Close with prayer. Then let kids enjoy their cookies.

FEATURE ME

Instructions: Have different people sign each blank according to which body part they think is your best feature.

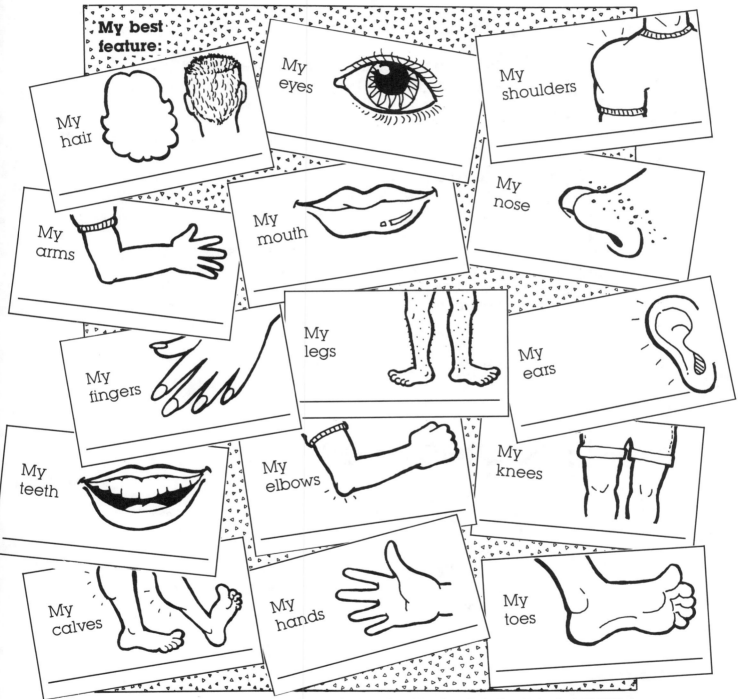

My best feature:

My hair

My eyes

My shoulders

My arms

My mouth

My nose

My fingers

My legs

My ears

My teeth

My elbows

My knees

My calves

My hands

My toes

Sex: God's Good Gift

A fifth-grade Sunday school teacher overheard this conversation:

"Did you see that new guy?" whispered Sarah to Emily. "He's really hot. And he was watching you in church."

"It's no big deal," Emily quickly responded. "His name is Justin. He goes to my school and he's already going out with Suzanne, 'Miss Popularity.' She got her hands on him right away. She moves fast."

On the other side of the room, three boys were listening to the girls' chatter. Mark leaned over to Chad and asked, "What are those girls yappin' about now? They're always whispering about something. Girls are so stupid."

Kids develop physically at different rates. Elementary-age girls may begin to get interested in guys while the guys may not even think twice about girls. Even among same-sex kids, the changes that accompany puberty come at different times. It can be a hard time for kids—whether they're early bloomers or late bloomers.

In this meeting, you'll help kids understand their sexuality and accept themselves as they are.

Objectives

In this meeting, elementary kids will:
- compare what they're like now to when they were babies;
- see how God is intimately involved in their physical development;
- discuss the Bible's view of sexual sin; and
- play a game that illustrates the pressures of growing up too soon.

by
Margaret
Hinchey

The Meeting

1 Baby names

(Before the meeting, ask kids to each bring a baby photo of themselves. Ask them to each write their name in pencil on the back of the photo without showing it to anyone else. Ask parents to remind kids to bring the photos. You'll need a bulletin board, tape or tacks, and numbered slips of paper. For each person, you'll need pink or blue construction paper, tape and a marker.)

As kids enter, have an adult volunteer collect their photos. Instruct the volunteer to tape or tack the photos on a bulletin board and label them with numbered slips of paper.

Have kids each make a name tag with pink or blue construction paper—pink for girls, blue for guys. Ask them to each print the name they like to be called now in big letters on the name tag. Then ask them to each print their nickname as a baby in smaller letters. For example, Elizabeth might write "Beth" in big letters and "Little Bit" in smaller letters. Have kids each tape their name tag to their clothes.

Have kids form a circle. Have them each tell the nickname they were called as a baby.

Ask those still called by their baby nickname:
- **Why are you still called by your baby nickname?**

Ask those whose nicknames have changed:
- **Why aren't you called by your baby nickname anymore?**

Say: **As we grow, our preferences usually change. What was okay for you when you were a baby may be embarrassing now. Let's see how else we've changed over the years.**

2 Baby faces

(You'll need the baby-photo bulletin board and a few giant lollipops. For each person, you'll need a sheet of paper and a pencil.)

Give kids each a sheet of paper and a pencil. Have kids number their papers according to the number of baby photos on the bulletin board. Identify kids who didn't bring photos, if any. Let those kids participate, but warn other kids that none of the pictures are of those kids.

Have kids quietly go to the bulletin board and decide who's in each photo. Let kids laugh, but don't allow them to yell out names or pick on each other. Remind the group that the person who correctly guesses the most names will win a prize.

After about five minutes, call time. Then, one by one, read aloud the name on the back of each photo. Have kids each check their own answer sheet. Award giant lollipops to kids who have the most correct answers.

3 The times they are a changin'

(You'll need a Bible, newsprint, tape and a marker.)

Tape a sheet of newsprint to the wall. Ask kids to each think about their baby photo and decide what's changed about them since they were a baby. List kids' responses on the newsprint. Use these suggestions to help kids get started:

● More hair;
● Less baby fat;
● More differences between guys and girls; and
● More intelligence.

Review the list. Then read aloud Psalm 139:15-16. Ask:

● **Why do you think God takes such care to plan your physical growth?**

Say: **Your physical changes are all part of God's great plan for you. Puberty, the period of time when you become sexually mature, has either begun or is coming for each of you. But even though you may not understand all that happens to you physically, be assured that God cares about you and is in complete control.**

4 God never changes

(You'll need a Bible.)

Say: **As we grow up physically, everything in and around us may seem to be changing. But we know who we can always count on to never change—God. God never changes, and his plans for us never change either. God gave us a message through the Bible about our sexuality. Let's listen to those words.**

Read aloud 1 Corinthians 6:18-20. Ask:
- **What do you think God means by these words?**
- **Why is it good to obey God when it comes to our bodies?**

Say: **God knows that as you develop physically, you'll be tempted to do things with your body that make God sad. So God tells us in the Bible what behaviors are wrong so we can know how to make good choices about our sexuality.**

5 Spin the bottle

(You'll need a soft-drink bottle and a basket. Photocopy, cut apart and fold the slips from the "Spin the Bottle" handout on page 41, and place the slips in the basket.)

Have kids sit on the floor in a circle. Hold up the soft-drink bottle and the basket of paper slips. Say: **We're going to play a special version of Spin the Bottle. I'll put this soft-drink bottle in the center of the circle. I'll spin the bottle and wait for it to point to someone. The person the bottle points to must draw a slip of paper from the basket and follow the instructions on the slip of paper.**

Spin the bottle to start the game. Allow kids to "pass" if they feel uncomfortable, but strongly encourage them to do what the slip of paper says. Continue to play until everyone has had at least one turn.

After the game, ask:
- **How'd you feel playing this game?**
- **Did you enjoy following the instructions? Why or why not?**

Say: **I strongly encouraged you to do what the slips of paper instructed, even if you didn't want to. In the same way, you might feel pressure to fit in "physically" with your friends. But instead of trying to be like everyone else, it's best to relax and be yourself. God loves you just as you are. And he has a perfect plan for your sexual development.**

6 A time for thanks

(No supplies needed.)

Ask kids to stand and join hands in the circle. Tell them to follow your motions as you say the following prayer.

God, we praise you for the gifts of your creation. (Raise joined hands and move toward the center of the circle.)

We thank you for who we are as individuals. (Keep hands joined, but lower them and move back toward the outside of the circle.)

We thank you for giving us knowledge about our bodies. (Raise joined hands and move toward the center of the circle.)

Help us be wise and avoid making you sad by disobeying your Word. (Keep hands joined, but lower them and move back toward the outside of the circle.)

Help us to live as your holy people. (Raise joined hands and move toward the center of the circle.)

Let God's holy people say, "amen!" (Break hands loose and give those around you "high fives.")

7 A time for snacks

(For each person, you'll need a healthy snack such as a granola bar and fruit juice.)

Serve healthy snacks to celebrate God's goodness toward kids. Remind kids to use their sexuality wisely and to take care of all parts of their bodies for God's glory.

Spin the Bottle

Instructions: Photocopy, cut apart and fold these slips, and place them in a basket.

- ✂ - - -

Pat someone on the back and say, "You did a good job today."

- ✂ - - -

Shake hands with the leader.

- ✂ - - -

Put on lipstick.

- ✂ - - -

Sing "Happy Birthday" to yourself.

- ✂ - - -

Hug someone you like.

- ✂ - - -

Pretend to be a frog.

- ✂ - - -

Do a somersault.

- ✂ - - -

Pretend to be a body-builder posing for a contest.

- ✂ - - -

Give a back rub to someone who looks tired.

- ✂ - - -

Tell your most embarrassing moment.

- ✂ - - -

Kiss a friend on the elbow.

- ✂ - - -

On Your Mark, Get Set, Go!

Kids are always competing—in school for grades, outside with games, or at home for attention or love. Our society tells them they have to be "first" or "best" to be important. The push-and-pull of competition influences kids' self-concepts.

In our race toward heaven, children need to understand that earthly competition isn't that important. But the race toward heaven—staying on the path for Christ and following God's will—is what really matters.

Objectives

In this meeting, elementary kids will:
● compete in crazy relays;
● see that they're valuable whether they win or lose;
● learn that competition can be negative; and
● discover the importance of running the Christian race.

The Meeting

1 Winning and losing

(You'll need newsprint, tape and a marker. For each person, you'll need a marker.)

Tape a sheet of newsprint to the wall. Draw a line down the middle of the newsprint. On one side, write "winning" and draw a happy face beside it. On the other side, write "losing" and draw a sad face beside it. Give kids each a marker and have them list ways they've won or lost this past week. For example, kids might write "I won my basketball game" or "I lost my homework."

Review kids' responses. Say: **Although we feel good when we win, it's easy to feel sad when we lose. It's especially hard**

by
Janel Kauffman

to feel good about ourselves when we do our best and still don't come out on top. Today we'll be talking about winning and losing, and how Jesus feels about competition.

2 Who's really the winner?

(You'll need a bag of Hershey's Kisses and a Bible. Number four different sets of paper slips from 1 to 3. Place the numbered slips in a bowl. Label the bowl "Point Bowl.")

Form three teams. Have teams do the relays described in the box below. As each relay is completed, rank the teams first, second and third. Draw a slip of paper from the point bowl. The team whose ranking corresponds to the number on the slip

Relay Descriptions

Relay 1

Have teams each stand in a line and pass a ball between their legs. When the last person has the ball, have him or her run to the front of the line and begin passing the ball back again. The relay is complete when the first person is back in front.

Relay 2

Have teams each stand in a line and pass an orange under their chins. The relay is complete when the orange reaches the end of the line.

Relay 3

Have teams each stand in a line at one end of the room. Have team members each place an unshelled peanut on their nose and walk to a chair on the opposite side of the room, circle it and return without dropping the peanut. The relay is complete when each team member has completed the course.

Relay 4

Have teams each stand in a line and pass a feather down the line by blowing it up in the air to the next person. The relay is complete when the feather reaches the end of the line.

of paper gets 1,000 points. For example, if you draw the number 3 from the point bowl, the team that placed third in that relay gets 1,000 points. The other two teams get no points.

When all four relays are completed, add up the points for each team and announce a winner.

After each relay, draw a number from the point bowl and award the appropriate team with 1,000 points. When all four relays are finished, tally the points and announce the winner. Celebrate by giving the winning team members each a Hershey's Kiss. Then call everyone together and ask:

● **How'd you feel as we played these games?**

● **Did you think the relays were unfair? Why or why not?**

Say: **In the relays, the points weren't always awarded to the winning team. It's like that in life too. Sometimes you don't get recognized by others even though you're just as important as those who do get recognized.**

Read aloud Matthew 20:16. Say: **Being first at something doesn't always make you a winner. And not being the "best" doesn't mean you aren't a winner. God doesn't just measure you by your abilities. He judges you by who you are on the inside.**

3 | Sportsmanship situations

(You'll need a Bible.)

Form two groups. Tell each group one of the following situations to discuss and act out in front of the other group. Tell kids they must each participate in their group's situation.

Situation 1

Act out a scene where one person always wants to win and gets very upset at any loss.

Situation 2

Act out a scene where a non-athletic person isn't allowed to play because the team doesn't want to lose.

After the situations are acted out, commend each group. Then ask:

● **How'd you feel about the characters in these scenes?**

● **Which character do you think you're most like?**

● **How would you respond if you were in these situations?**

● **How do you think Jesus would've responded in these situations?**

Say: **Competition can be hard when others are cruel to you or when you don't do as well as you'd like. But Jesus never** treats you like a loser. He always sees you as a winner.

Read aloud 2 Timothy 4:7-8. Say: **If you believe in Jesus, then God believes in you. He thinks you're special! Even when you lose a race or a game, Jesus still thinks you're worthy of the victorious "crown of righteousness."**

4 | Win the crown

(You'll need a recording of the theme from *Rocky* and a stereo. For each person, you'll need an 11×17-inch sheet of construction paper, a marker, tape, scissors and a pencil.)

Give kids each an 11×17-inch sheet of construction paper, a marker, tape and scissors. Say: **With your supplies, create a "crown of righteousness" for yourself. Write your name on your crown, and leave space on your crown for others to write in.**

When everyone is finished, give kids each a pencil. Have kids each write on each person's crown one "winning quality" they see in that person. For example, kids might write "you make me laugh" or "you're always nice." When everyone is finished, allow kids time to read their crowns.

Collect all the crowns. Play a recording of the theme from *Rocky*. While the music is playing, crown each person with his or her creation.

Stop the music and say: **We all have God-given qualities that help make us "winners" in the race for God. Before we close, let's energize our bodies for the race ahead.**

5 | Running snacks

(You'll need a Bible. For each person, you'll need a granola bar or a piece of fruit.)

Have kids form a circle. Give kids each a granola bar or a piece of fruit.

Read aloud Hebrews 12:1-2. Say: **Competition can be good in life, as long as your reason is to improve yourself and not to make someone else feel like a loser. Don't let others distract you from your ultimate race—the race to be like Jesus.**

Close with prayer, asking God to strengthen kids' hearts to run the Christian race with endurance. Then turn the music back on and let kids enjoy their snacks.

Choices, Choices Everywhere!

As kids move through their elementary school years, a world of choices opens up for them. Kids begin to choose what clothes to wear, what music to listen to and what friends to have. And they begin to make choices that could affect their future—positively or negatively. For this reason, kids need to learn to make responsible decisions.

Use this meeting to help kids practice making simple decisions. Children will see that choices have consequences, and they'll discover that God is there to help them make wise decisions.

Objectives

In this meeting, elementary kids will:
● practice making decisions;
● look at the pros and cons of choices;
● examine the choices made by Bible characters; and
● see that God is always with them to help them make good decisions.

The Meeting

1 Taste test

(You'll need an assortment of drinks such as Coca-Cola, Pepsi, Sprite, 7Up, Dr. Pepper, water, iced tea, juice and Kool-Aid. You'll also need an assortment of candy bars such as Milky Way, Snickers, Hershey's, Heath and Butterfinger. Include some granola bars and fruit bars. You'll also need napkins, cups and ice.)

by
Kelli Woodall

Set out the drinks and treats. Have kids come up one at a time and choose their refreshments. Let kids enjoy the treats. When everyone is finished, ask:

- **Did you enjoy your snacks? Why or why not?**
- **How'd you choose what you'd have?**
- **Were some items better for you than others?**

Say: **Today we're going to talk about making choices. We'll look at why it's important to make good choices. And we'll learn that the decisions we make now can affect us in the future.**

2 The choosing game

(No supplies needed.)

Play the Choosing Game on page 48. After the game, have kids return to their seats. Then ask:

- **How'd you feel as you played this game?**
- **What was fun or exciting about this game?**

Say: **In the game, every time you made a choice, it caused you to either move or stay where you were. It's like that in real life too. The choices you make determine where you'll be and the kind of life you'll live. Let's look at real-life situations and practice our decision-making skills.**

3 Pros and cons

(You'll need newsprint, tape and a marker.)

Use the "Pros and Cons" situations on page 49 for this activity. Form two groups—a "pro" group and a "con" group. Tape a sheet of newsprint to the wall. Read aloud each situation. Have the pros tell why the person in the situation made the right decision. Then have the cons tell why the person in the situation made a bad decision. Then have groups work together to come up with an alternative solution for each situation. List kids' solutions on newsprint.

Commend groups in their decision-making skills. Then say: **As you can tell, even right decisions don't fully solve problems. That's why you need to think and pray about the decisions you make, so you'll know you're doing what's best in every situation.**

Choosing Game

Instructions: Have kids sit on chairs in a circle. Read each of the following statements one at a time. For each statement, have kids follow the instructions it gives. Kids will end up sitting on top of each other in the circle.

Move one chair to the right if . . .

1. you like math better than English.

2. you'd rather talk to your mother than your father about a problem.

3. you prefer to wear red T-shirts instead of blue T-shirts.

4. you like curly hair better than straight hair.

5. you'd rather go to the beach than the mountains.

6. you'd rather go to the movies than skating.

7. you like Pepsi better than Coca-Cola.

8. you prefer hamburgers to pizza.

9. you like pepperoni pizza more than cheese pizza.

10. you like chocolate ice cream better than vanilla ice cream.

11. you'd rather play baseball than basketball.

12. you'd rather watch sports than play sports.

13. you like comedy TV shows better than action TV shows.

14. you'd rather stay up late than get up early.

15. you like cats more than dogs.

16. you'd rather learn to play a musical instrument than listen to somebody else play.

17. you'd rather your friend tell you the truth than protect your feelings.

18. you like advice from friends more than from your parents.

19. you'd rather spend time with your brother or sister than your friends.

20. you trust your grandparents more than your teachers.

Pros and Cons

Situation 1
Amy and Julie have been best friends for years. Amy is also friends with Karen. As Amy's birthday party approaches, Julie insists that Karen can't be invited. She says that if Amy invites Karen, she won't come to the party.

Amy decides to go along with Julie and leave Karen out.

Situation 2
Danny goes camping with Steve and his father. Steve's father leaves the boys at the campsite to go fishing downstream. A young man comes up and says he's hungry and asks the boys for something to eat.

Danny says "sure" and asks the fellow to join them.

Situation 3
Dawnice hasn't missed a single meeting of her elementary church group. The group is preparing for a special program they'll present soon to the congregation. Dawnice is excited about playing one of the main parts. Mitch, who she really likes, calls and asks her to go with him and his parents to the movies. It'll mean missing practice.

She decides to go with Mitch to the movies.

4 Character decisions

(Photocopy, cut apart and fold the cards from the "Character Choices" handout on pages 51 and 52. You'll need a Bible.)

Have kids stay in their groups. Say: **Let's look at more situations, only these are all real situations experienced by people in the Bible. Let's see how our choices compare with those made by Bible people.**

Call on a volunteer to read aloud side A of the first card from the "Character Choices" cards.

Have the pros and cons groups discuss what each biblical character should do. Then have the volunteer flip over the card and read the biblical character's identity and the choice he made. Then read aloud the Bible passage that relates to the card.

Repeat the process for all the cards, using a different volunteer each time. After all the cards have been discussed, ask:

● Was it hard to decide what to do in these situations? Why or why not?

● What helped you decide what was best?

Say: **When making decisions, remember God's involvement in your situations. Ask God to help you make good decisions. And he'll guide you to do what's best for you and for those around you.**

5 Prayer cards

(For each person, you'll need a 3×5 card and a pencil.)

Give kids each a 3×5 card and a pencil. Have kids each write one "tough choice" they have to make. It could be anything from deciding which club to join at school to which parent they should live with. When kids are finished, form pairs and have partners each tell what they wrote. Then have partners trade cards.

Call everyone together and say: **Take your partner's card home with you. Tonight, before you go to bed, take out the card and pray for God to help your partner make a good decision about that situation.**

Remind children that God is always with them when they make choices. Close with prayer, asking God to help kids make wise decisions.

Character Choices

Instructions: Photocopy, cut apart and fold these cards to use in activity 4.

Card 1

Side A

I am truly a man of God. The king liked me so much he gave me lots of power and responsibility. The other men in the kingdom got jealous and tricked the king into passing a law they knew I'd break. The law was passed. It would mean being disobedient to God to live by that law. But if I don't uphold the law I'll be sentenced to very severe punishment.

What should I do?

FOLD HERE

Side B

Daniel 6:6-7,10
My name is Daniel.
Choice: I decided to pray at my window three times a day as I always had, even though it was now against the law.
Consequence: I was thrown in the lion's den.
God's involvement: God shut the lion's mouths and saved me. Then the king made it a law to follow my God.

Card 2

Side A

I am a great man of God. God made me big promises. He gave me the most wonderful gift. I had prayed for it for many years. Then God told me to give my great gift away. In fact, I was to destroy it. How can I destroy this gift I love? After all, God gave it to me.

What should I do?

FOLD HERE

Side B

Genesis 22:9-12
My name is Abraham.
Choice: God promised me a son. I was very old when Isaac was born. Then God asked me to sacrifice Isaac. I agreed.
Consequence: I built the altar and bound my son. I really thought I was going to have to do it.
God's involvement: God stopped me just in the nick of time. He rewarded me in great ways for my faithfulness.

continued

Card 3

Side A

God thought of me as a son. He was angry at a lot of people. He told me to build a boat so I could hide from his fury. Everybody thought I was crazy and laughed at me. Maybe I should quit.

What should I do?

FOLD HERE

Side B

Genesis 6:11-14, 22

My name is Noah.

Choice: God told me to build a great ark. I trusted his word and built the ark.

Consequence: Boy am I glad I trusted him. There was a great big flood. Because I was in that ark, I was saved.

God's involvement: God saved me because I was faithful to him.

Card 4

Side A

I was minding my own business when God told me to go tell some strangers he was upset with them. Would you go tell strangers "God is mad at you"? If I go, they'll think I'm stupid.

What should I do?

FOLD HERE

Side B

Jonah 1:1-3

My name is Jonah.

Choice: God told me to go to Nineveh. I tried to run away.

Consequence: I ended up in the belly of a big fish. Three days later, after I prayed and apologized for my sin, God saved me. I ended up going to Nineveh anyway. And God's will was done.

God's involvement: God made it difficult to run away from him. It's best to obey when God tells you to do something.

Card 5

Side A

I was sent by God on a huge mission. After 33 years of hard work in his name, the time came for me to make a huge choice. I was asked to give my life to save other people.

What should I do?

FOLD HERE

Side B

Luke 22:39-44

My name is Jesus.

Choice: I asked God not to have me die on the cross. But I also told him if it was his will I'd do it.

Consequence: Because I went through that painful death, you have the opportunity to accept God's gift of eternal life. All you have to do is believe in what I've done for you and receive my forgiveness for your sins.

God's involvement: As usual, God had a big plan. Because I was faithful, you can have eternal life.

When I Grow Up

One question every child hears is "What do you want to be when you grow up?" From early on, kids are impressed with the need to be concerned about the future.

Christian kids actually need to hear another question: "Who do you want to be when you grow up?" They need to understand that God isn't just concerned about their vocations; he's most concerned about their character. God wants kids to grow up to be like Jesus.

Use this meeting to help kids think about the kind of people they want to be when they grow up.

Objectives

In this meeting, elementary kids will:
● create wardrobe items that describe vocations they'll have;
● add inner qualities to their wardrobes;
● decide which character qualities they most want to invest their lives in; and
● see that God is more concerned with who they become than what they become.

The Meeting

1 Just wait

(You'll need the following nacho-cheese ingredients: 1 pound of cooked hamburger, a small chopped onion, 1 pound of cubed Velveeta Cheese and a medium-size can of Rotel Tomatoes. You'll also need a crock pot.)

Set out 1 pound of cooked hamburger, a small chopped onion, 1 pound of cubed Velveeta Cheese, and an opened

by
Christine Yount

medium-size can of Rotel Tomatoes. Ask:

● **Who'll volunteer to eat all of this food as it is?**

Stress that the volunteer must eat all of the food in its current state. Probably no one will volunteer.

Say: **Even if someone would volunteer, I wouldn't let you eat this food like this because it isn't finished yet.**

Take out a crock pot and plug it in. As you add the food to the crock pot, say: **This food looks okay now, but it'll be even better when it's finished. While we have our meeting, this food will be cooking. And we'll enjoy it in its final state.**

As you smell the food cooking, think about how God isn't finished with you yet either. God is working with you every day to make you who he wants you to be.

Stir the mixture occasionally throughout the meeting to be sure the cheese melts evenly.

2 Design a wardrobe

(You'll need a Bible. For each person, you'll need a sheet of newsprint, scissors, tape and a marker.)

Give kids each a sheet of newsprint, scissors, tape and a marker. Have them each create a wardrobe item that shows what they'll be doing when they grow up. Encourage kids to create items that show careers they'll have, whether they'll be married or whether they'll have children. For example, kids could make ties, aprons or nurse's caps.

When everyone is finished, have kids put their items on. Have them each explain their wardrobe item. Congratulate kids on their creativity.

Read aloud Colossians 3:12-14. Say: **God cares about your future—what kind of work you'll do, where you'll live and what your life will be like. But God is most concerned about the kind of person you become. Will you grow up to be mean and cranky or kind and caring?**

Give kids newsprint and markers. Say: **On your newsprint, create three symbols that represent the kind of person you want to become. For example, you might draw a heart to represent "loving" or a dollar bill to represent "generous."**

Read aloud Colossians 3:12-14 again to give kids suggestions. When everyone is finished, have kids each tape their symbols to their clothes. Then have kids each explain their symbols. Ask:

● **Was this activity hard? Why or why not?**

Say: **Just as you added the symbols to your clothes, so God wants to add Christ's qualities to your life as you grow.**

Ask:

● **How do you feel when you think about the future? Explain.**

● **Why is it good to know that God is in control of our future?**

Say: **God is love. Although he cares about what you do with your life, he is most concerned with how you love others. You could be very rich or famous, but if you don't love others, God won't be pleased. Or you could be very poor and not well-known, but as long as you love like Jesus loves, God will be pleased with you.**

3 ◁ Character store

(Photocopy and cut apart the "Character-Quality Money" handout on page 57. Make enough copies so each person will have a total of $70 in play money. Photocopy the "Character-Quality Price List" on page 58 and tape it to a wall. If you have more than 12 kids, make more copies and tape them around the room. For each person, you'll need a sheet of paper and a pencil.)

Have kids each remove their symbols. Give kids each a sheet of paper, a pencil and 14 play-money bills. Point out the price list on the wall.

Say: **I'm the storekeeper of the Character-Quality Store. You've each been given $70—that's $1 for each year you may live. You must decide which qualities from the list you'd like to have. Write each quality you choose on your paper, along with its price. Remember, you can't spend more than $70. When you've chosen all your qualities, come to me and pay what you owe.**

Have kids shop for the qualities they consider most important. Remind kids to each "check out." Collect their play money and pray aloud for each person to receive the qualities they purchased; for example, "God, bless Bobby with a loving heart and the ability to be patient."

After everyone has checked out, ask:

● **Why are the qualities you chose important to you?**

● **How can you act out those qualities in your life?**

Say: **God has special plans for each of us. He knows what career you'll choose, whether you'll marry and how many kids you'll have. God wants you to be happy and to have a good** life. But more than anything, God wants you to act like Jesus. He's working in you every day to help you live your life as Jesus would.

4 Résumés

(For each person, you'll need a pencil and a "Résumé" handout on page 59.)

Say: **Let's put together all we've learned about our dreams and God's desires and create a résumé. A résumé is a brief description of a person's life and history.**

Form groups of three. Give a "Résumé" handout and a pencil to each person. In their groups, have kids work together to create a résumé for each person in the group. Circulate to help groups as needed.

When groups are finished, call everyone together and have kids each explain their résumé.

Say: **Take your résumé home and tape it to your bedroom mirror or door. Read it often to remind yourself of all the exciting things God has in store for your future.**

5 Dip into the future

(You'll need the crock pot of nacho cheese from activity 1 and a ladle. You'll also need a bowl, napkins and tortilla chips for each person.)

Set out bowls, napkins and tortilla chips and the now-ready nacho cheese. Help kids each ladle nacho cheese over the tortilla chips in their bowl. As kids enjoy the snack, say: **This snack might've tasted okay at the beginning of the meeting, but it tastes much better now. Our lives are like that too. God enjoys who we are now, but he knows we'll just keep getting better and better as we grow up and learn to act more like Jesus.**

Close with prayer, thanking God for his plan for kids' lives.

Character-Quality Money

Instructions: Photocopy and cut apart these play-money bills. Make enough so each person can have $70.

Character-Quality
Price List

Instructions: Choose which qualities you want to purchase, then write the qualities and their prices on your paper. Remember, you can't spend more than $70.

Love $50

Joy $35

Peace..$35

Patience $20

Kindness...$20

Goodness...$20

Faithfulness.......................................$20

Gentleness...$20

Behaving right $20

Caring for others $25

Knowing right from wrong $10

Honesty $15

Sale!

Hurry!!
Sale
ends soon!

Résumé

Instructions: Work as a team to fill out a résumé for each person in your group. Imagine what each person will be like in 20 years.

HI!

My name is:

Career

Character qualities

Family members

Special interests or hobbies

No More Sesame Street!

Move over, Sesame Street! Here comes MTV!
Say goodbye to Barbie Dolls. Now kids want Young
Miss or Seventeen magazine. Studies show that kids
are growing up faster today than ever before. They're more
sophisticated and more culture-smart.

But they each still have a child's heart.

Elementary children are on the edge of becoming adults.
Some have already "sprouted" physically. Some see their peers
doing "adult" things, such as smoking and drinking. But deep
down, kids are still kids. And they need guidance to handle
their newfound independence responsibly.

In this meeting, kids will discuss the new independence they
have. They'll discover that independence brings responsibility.
And they'll learn to handle that responsibility well.

Objectives

In this meeting, elementary kids will:
● play a game about growing up;
● talk about Jesus growing up;
● discuss ways they're becoming more independent; and
● affirm that they are each special to God.

The Meeting

1 Growing-up relay

(For each team of five or fewer, you'll need a
broom, a dictionary, a bowl of popcorn, a soft drink, a
blanket, a diploma and a small bowl of uncooked rice. Pile all
the teams' items in one pile in a corner of the room. Photocopy
and cut apart the relay instructions from the "Relay! Relay!"
handout on page 64. Make a set of instructions for each team.)

by
Rick Chromey

Because this lesson is on independence, allow kids to create their own teams of five or fewer. The only guideline is kids must have at least one member of the opposite sex on their team (this is necessary for one portion of the relay). Once teams are formed, have them each line up 10 feet from the "activity pile" of items you prepared.

Tell teams they're going to play a fun game about growing up and they must carefully follow the relay instructions you'll give them. The team that successfully completes all six instructions first wins.

Give teams each a set of relay instructions and tell them that each team member must participate in at least one relay. When everyone is ready, start the relay.

Award the winning team members each with a firm "grown-up" handshake and a "congratulations."

2 Growing-up time

(For each person, you'll need a Bible.)

After the relay, bring everyone together and give each child a Bible. Say: **Growing up and becoming more independent is something everyone has to go through. Even Jesus had to learn to live away from his parents.**

Guide kids to look up Luke 2:41-42. Have a volunteer read the scripture aloud while kids read silently. Ask:

● **What are some things you and your family do every Christmas?**

● **What about on Easter? on your birthday?**

Say: **Jesus' parents also had a yearly tradition. Every Passover, they'd go to Jerusalem for the festival. But the festival was only for adults. When Jesus was 12, he was finally old enough to go along.**

Take the young people outside of the building, and have them play a game of Hide and Seek. You be "It." After the game, call everyone together outside and have a volunteer read aloud Luke 2:43-45. Ask:

● **Have you ever gotten lost? When?**

● **How does it feel to be lost?**

Say: **Even though Jesus was separated from his parents, he didn't feel lost. He was becoming a man and was feeling more comfortable about being away from his mother and father.**

Bring the group back into the classroom. Have another

volunteer read aloud Luke 2:46-50. Say: **Mary and Joseph were surprised that Jesus didn't leave Jerusalem when they did. They were beginning to see that Jesus wasn't a little boy anymore. He could make decisions on his own.**

3 Look at me now

(You'll need a Bible, newsprint and tape. For each person, you'll need a marker.)

Read aloud Luke 2:52. Tape a sheet of newsprint to each wall. Write a different one of these headings on each newsprint: Wisdom—making good decisions; Stature—growing up physically; Favor with God—getting to know God; and Favor with people—getting to know others.

Give each child a marker. Under each newsprint heading, have kids each write one way they're becoming more independent or "grown up" in that area. Encourage kids to answer as specifically as possible. To help kids get started, give an example for each heading, such as:

- Wisdom—I can buy my own clothes.
- Stature—I'm getting taller.
- Favor with God—I go to Sunday school.
- Favor with people—I play baseball with my friends.

Discuss kids' responses. Point out other ways kids' lives will be changing. Say: **As you grow and change, you'll be allowed to make more decisions on your own. And the older you get, the more responsible you are for what you do.**

4 Independently special

(For each person, you'll need a photocopy of the "Independently Special" handout on page 65, scissors and a pencil.)

Give kids each an "Independently Special" handout, scissors and a pencil. Have kids each read the instructions, then list one thing they enjoy or can do that makes them special; for example, "I can draw" or "I speak two languages." Then have kids each write one way they want to be more independent; for example, "I want to stay out after school" or "I want to spend the night at my friend's house more often."

Have kids each cut out their card. Say: **Place your card in** your wallet, purse or school notebook as a reminder that you're "independently special."

5 | Unique snacks

(For each person, you'll need a snack that's unique, such as popcorn or raisins.)

Give kids each a snack that's unique, such as popcorn or raisins. While kids enjoy the treats, say: **Just as each snack is unique, each of you is unique in God's eyes. And God wants to help you grow up into the special person he's planned for you to be. As you learn to do more things by yourself, remember you're never totally alone. God is always with you.**

Close with prayer, thanking God for helping kids grow up and for never leaving them alone.

Relay! Relay!

Instructions: Photocopy and cut apart a set of these instructions for each team of five or fewer.

---- ✂ ----

Relay 1
Run to the broom, place the handle to your forehead and run around the broom five times. When you're finished, shout, "Growing up makes me dizzy!"

---- ✂ ----

Relay 2
Run to the dictionary. Look up the word "school," and read aloud the definition.

---- ✂ ----

Relay 3
Run and eat the bowl of popcorn and drink the soft drink, then say, "Party, party, party!"

---- ✂ ----

Relay 4
Have another member of your team drag a fellow teammate around the room on a blanket while the person being dragged says three times, "New car, new license, new fun!"

---- ✂ ----

Relay 5
Run and write your name on the fake diploma and say, "School's done, school's done, now it's time for lotsa fun!"

---- ✂ ----

Relay 6
Have a girl and a guy on your team link arms, run to the bowl of rice, throw rice into the air and say, "We've only just begun!"

---- ✂ ----

Independently Special!

Instructions:

As we've learned in today's meeting, YOU'RE growing up! You're becoming more independent! But becoming more independent brings responsibility. Fill out the "Independently Special" card, then cut it out and place it in your billfold, purse or school notebook to remind you that you're special to God.

Independently Special!

I'm unique because:

_____

_____

One way I want to be more independent is:

_____

_____

Signed: _____

Part 3
My Friends

True Friends

*"**F**riends are friends forever, if the Lord's the Lord of them."*
The dark concert hall echoes with hundreds of voices as Michael W. Smith leads the young audience in song.
"And a friend will not say 'never,' for the welcome will not end."

Kids of all ages—from high school all the way down to elementary school—join hands and raise them high in tribute to the joys of friendship. They know the words by heart. Everyone is caught up in the moment. In the end, a lone spotlight focuses on a cross behind the stage.

"No, a lifetime's not too long to live as friends."

Elementary kids experience the importance of friendship. Friendship means the difference between eating with others in the lunchroom and eating alone. It's the difference between standing alone in a fight and having a friend beside you to back you up.

Friends are important to kids. In this meeting, you'll help elementary kids learn what it means to be true friends and see how they can improve their friendship skills.

Objectives

In this meeting, elementary kids will:
- find things in common with others in the group;
- see how friends should "stick" together;
- understand what it means to be a true friend; and
- apply the golden rule to their friendships.

The Meeting

1 Identification tags

(For each person, you'll need three blank sticky labels and a pencil.)

by
Esther M. Bailey

Give kids each three blank sticky labels and a pencil. Have kids each write their name on one label; their favorite interest, such as fishing, baseball or baton-twirling, on the second label; and what they want to be when they grow up on the third label. Have kids each stick their labels to their clothes.

Have kids circulate around the room until they find partners who have similar interests or common career goals. Have kids each tell their partner three things about themselves that their partner doesn't already know; for example, "I've been to Canada" or "I had an operation when I was a baby." When pairs are finished, have kids each introduce their partner and tell what they learned about him or her. Ask:

● **You and your partner have similar interests or goals. Does that mean you're just alike? Why or why not?**

● **What's different about you?**

● **Would you rather spend time with someone just like you or someone different? Explain.**

● **Why is finding out about others so much fun?**

Say: **We enjoy learning about others because that's how we make new friends. And friends are good to have because they make life more fun and help us when we have problems.**

2 Stick together

(For each person, you'll need a 2-foot strip of masking tape.)

Have kids form a circle. Give kids each a 2-foot strip of masking tape. Say: **Wrap one end of the tape around your wrist. Then wrap the other end around the wrist of one other person in the room who's your friend.**

Watch kids tape themselves to each other. Some will tape themselves to a partner so the two of them will be by themselves. Others will create a giant web of tape that connects several kids. Allow kids to tape themselves however they want, but don't allow them to waste tape or divert their attention from the activity.

After everyone is connected, ask:

● **How does it feel to be taped together?**

● **Why is it good to have friends?**

Say: **Friends are good to have because they "stick" by you no matter what. Just as this tape sticks you to your friends, so you and your friends should stick together even if you don't always get along.**

3 Scripture friendships

(You'll need a Bible and three copies of the "Scripture Skits" handout on page 73.)

Form three groups and assign each group a separate skit from the "Scripture Skits" handout. Have adult volunteers work with each group to help them read through the skit, find props if needed, and assign parts. Have kids who don't have speaking parts become part of the set, such as chairs or trees.

When groups are ready, have them each perform their skit. After skit 1, ask:

● **How was Ruth a friend to Naomi in this story?**

● **How was Orpah not a friend to Naomi in this story?**

Read aloud Proverbs 18:24 and say: **Some friends only like you when you're popular or funny. They walk away whenever trouble comes. But Ruth stuck by Naomi's side even when it meant going through hard times. Ruth was a true friend.**

After skit 2, say: **Job's friends came to see him because he was unhappy. But when they came, they only made Job feel worse.** Ask:

● **How did Job's friends make Job feel worse about his situation?**

Read aloud Romans 2:1 and say: **Job's friends told Job he was the cause of his own problems. They didn't really try to encourage him or comfort him. True friends help each other when they're sad. A true friend will help you feel better, not tell you, "It's all your own fault."**

After skit 3, ask:

● **What should you do if one of your friends does something wrong?**

● **What did Jonathan want to do?**

Read aloud 2 Thessalonians 3:13 and say: **When someone is wrong, even if it's your friend, you need to stand up for what's right. Jonathan tried to get his father to do what was right. But Jonathan couldn't convince his father. So Jonathan stood up for what was right by helping David escape.**

After all the skits, say: **True friends stick by you in rough times, encourage you when you're sad and stand up for what's right even if others disagree.** Ask:

● **Do you know of someone who's your true friend? Who?**

● **Are you a true friend to someone? Who?**

● **How do you know you're a true friend?**

Say: **Let's look at four situations and see what it means to be a true friend in each one.**

4 | Friendships at stake

(Photocopy and cut apart the situations from the "Friendship at Stake" handout on page 75. You'll need four pencils.)

Form four groups. A group can be one person. Give each group a different situation from the "Friendship at Stake" handout and a pencil. Have groups each write suggestions for the characters in their situation.

When groups are ready, have them each read aloud their situation and tell what suggestions they made. Say: **The Bible gives us a rule for friendship that can always help us be true friends to others. Let's read it.**

5 | The golden rule

(You'll need a Bible. For each person, you'll need a marker and a wooden ruler that's been painted gold.)
Read aloud Luke 6:31. Ask:

● **What would you want a friend to do if you got sick? flunked a test? lost a pet?**

Say: **Whenever you're trying to decide how to treat a friend in a certain situation, ask yourself, "How would I want someone to treat me in this situation?"**

Give kids each a golden ruler and a marker. Have kids each write "The Golden Rule" on one side of the ruler and "Luke 6:31" on the other side. Say: **Take your ruler home and hang it on your bedroom wall. Every time you look at it, ask yourself whether you're being a true friend to others.**

6 | Closing snacks

(For each person, you'll need an Almond Joy or Mounds candy bar.)

Have kids form a circle and join hands. Close with prayer: **Dear God, thank you for giving us friends. Help us always live by the golden rule.**

After the prayer, serve Almond Joy or Mounds bars. Have kids each eat one half of their candy bar and give the other half to a friend.

Scripture Skits

Instructions: In your group, prepare your assigned skit to perform in front of the other groups.

BETHLEHEM
50 KM

Skit 1 (Ruth 1)

RUTH: Naomi, my dear mother-in-law, I've noticed you look sad these days.

NAOMI: There isn't much left for me in Moab anymore with my husband and sons gone.

ORPAH: Death has been hard on all of us.

NAOMI: I've been thinking a lot about Bethlehem. I guess I'm really homesick. I hear all is well there. They're expecting a good barley crop this year. I'm thinking about going back.

RUTH: We'll go with you.

NAOMI: Oh, would you? That would be wonderful! (The threesome begins to walk away, then Naomi stops.)

NAOMI: I've been thinking. You'd be as homesick in Bethlehem as I am in Moab. You must go back. (Ruth and Orpah start to cry. Naomi hugs and kisses them.)

ORPAH
AND RUTH: No! We want to go with you.

NAOMI: There's nothing for you in Bethlehem. Go back to your own people.

ORPAH: Yeah, I guess you're right. See ya'. (Orpah walks away, waving to Ruth and Naomi.)

RUTH: Please, please, don't make me go back. I want to go where you go. I want to serve the God you serve.

NAOMI: Bless you, my daughter. You'll be a comfort to me in my old age. May the Lord deal kindly with you.

continued

Skit 2 (Job 3—37)

JOB:	As you can see, things are getting worse. Not only have I lost my money and family, now these sores all over my body are driving me crazy.
FIRST FRIEND:	Well, you know God doesn't punish anyone unless it's deserved.
JOB:	But I haven't done anything wrong.
SECOND FRIEND:	You may not be aware of your sin, but God knows.
JOB:	No, I'm sure I've done nothing wrong. And I don't understand why God doesn't take away my problems.
THIRD FRIEND:	I think you must have a secret sin. You don't want to confess it, but you must—or God will continue to punish you.
JOB:	What kind of friends are you? You come here pretending to comfort me and you end up making me more miserable than ever. If any of you needed help, I'd encourage you. I'd tell you that God loves you and that I'm still your friend.

Skit 3 (1 Samuel 18:3; 20:1-42)

JONATHAN:	David, I promise I'll always be your friend. To prove it, I'm giving you my robe. (Gives robe to David.)
DAVID:	Thanks, Jonathan. You'll always be my friend too. I only wish your father didn't hate me so much.
JONATHAN:	Oh, I think I got that straightened out. He was jealous of you and even wanted to kill you. But I talked to him and told him how loyal you've been. He agreed with me and promised me he wouldn't kill you.
DAVID:	He told you that only because he knows you and I are friends. But I tell you, my life is in danger from your father.
JONATHAN:	Whatever I can do, I'll be glad to do it.
DAVID:	I'm supposed to have dinner with your father tomorrow, but I'm not going to. Make an excuse for me and see how he reacts. If he's angry, he may tell you how he feels about me. Then you can let me know.
JONATHAN:	I'll do as you say and get back with you. (David and Jonathan walk to opposite sides of the room, then return to meet in the center.)
JONATHAN:	You were right, David. My father is out to kill you. Go hide to protect yourself, and always remember that my friendship goes with you.
DAVID:	It's wonderful of you, Jonathan, to side with me against your own father.
JONATHAN:	You are right and he is wrong. I always want to be on the right side.

Friendship at Stake

Instructions: Photocopy and cut apart these situations to use in activity 4.

------------------------------- ✂ -------------------

Situation 1

Sixth-grader Roberta has moved to a new school where she doesn't fit in at all. With her short, plain hairstyle, she looks like a boy. That was fine in cowboy country where she lived before. But in the city, the girls have longer hair and dress more daintily. Some of the boys have even begun to tease her. Roberta has always been a good student, but now she feels so bad about herself that her grades are slipping.

How could you be a true friend to Roberta?

------------------------------- ✂ -------------------

Situation 2

Freddy, a guy in your class is in the hospital with cancer. Freddy's best friend won't go to the hospital because it'd be embarrassing not knowing what to do or say. You aren't close friends with Freddy, but you know who he is.

What can you do to be a true friend to Freddy?

------------------------------- ✂ -------------------

Situation 3

Over the summer, you become friends with Cindy, a girl your age who's confined to a wheelchair. When school starts, you want to help Cindy become a part of your group. But every time you try to include Cindy in a conversation or game, your friends find something else to do. One day your friends tell you to stop hanging around Cindy or they'll stop being your friends.

How can you be a true friend to your old friends and to Cindy?

------------------------------- ✂ -------------------

Situation 4

Working together doing lawns, you and James become good friends. Although James doesn't go to church, he seems nice.

One day James says to you, "Would you still be my friend if you knew my dad was in prison?"

You can tell James is really concerned about how you'll respond, so you try to make him feel better. "Sure. It's no problem," you say.

When your sister begins to date James' older brother, you wonder whether you should tell your sister what you know about James' dad.

How can you be a true friend to James and to your sister?

------------------------------- ✂ -------------------

There's Only One "You"!

Mitchell came home from school crying today. Charlie, the most popular guy in fifth grade, punched Mitchell at recess in front of everyone—just to see if Mitchell would fall down.

Mitchell didn't fall—at least not on the outside. But now, crying in his room, he's emotionally knocked out. He's angry he didn't hit Charlie back. But he's mostly just hurt. What will his friends think of him now? He can hear them already . . .

"Mitchell is a wimp! Mitchell is a wimp!"

Elementary-age kids are in transition. All of a sudden, what other kids think of them is important. Socially, that can be good. Kids begin to learn more from each other, and they adapt to each other.

If a child's peer group is a positive influence, fitting in is usually okay. If the peer group is a negative influence, however, fitting in is never okay.

Use this meeting to help kids see they're unique creations of God and that God wants them to maintain their uniqueness in a world of conformity.

Objectives

In this meeting, elementary kids will:
- form human puzzles to illustrate how they "fit" with others;
- learn what God says about them in the Bible;
- see how conforming to others' expectations makes them lose what makes them special; and
- celebrate their uniqueness.

by
Christine Yount

The Meeting

1 Human puzzles

(No supplies needed.)

Form groups of four. Have groups each go to a separate room and create a human puzzle by forming a design or picture with their bodies. Tell them they must all be touching each other in some way. For example, a group could make a pyramid, circle or tree.

Have all groups come back together after five minutes. One at a time, have groups go to the front of the room. Have the individuals in each human puzzle stand apart from each other and freeze in their poses, without forming their puzzle. Have volunteers from the rest of the groups try to put the puzzle together. If volunteers are successful, give them a big round of applause. If not, have the human puzzle put itself together.

Continue until groups each have formed their human puzzle. Then ask:

● **How'd you feel when your puzzle fit together? when it didn't?**

● **How important is it for you to "fit in" or get along with your friends?**

Say: **Fitting in can be good if we don't try to pretend to be someone we aren't. Just as each of you was a unique piece of the puzzle in this activity, each of you is a unique part of our group. You don't need to change to fit in. Today we're going to learn to celebrate who we are as individuals.**

2 God's view

(You'll need newsprint, tape, four different-color markers and four Bibles.)

Form four groups. Tape a sheet of newsprint to the wall. Give each group a different-color marker and a Bible.

Assign one of the following passages to each group: John 15:15; Acts 1:8; 1 Peter 2:9; and 1 John 3:1. Have groups each read their scripture aloud.

Then have groups each write on the newsprint what God says about them—graffiti style. Encourage groups to draw pictures and symbols to illustrate what God says. For example, a group may draw a handshake to illustrate that God is their friend.

After kids have finished, have them sit in a semicircle in front of the graffiti newsprint. Ask:

● **How does it make you feel to know that God is your friend?**

● **How does it make you feel to know you're God's special child?**

Say: **These scriptures also say we're God's priests and witnesses. Priests are people who pray to God for others. We do that whenever we pray for our friends. Witnesses are people who tell about what they've seen or heard. We are witnesses for God whenever we tell our friends about God or what God means to us.**

3 Clay people

(For each person, you'll need a clump of different-color clay.)

Say: **God has made us each unique. That's why we're each so special to him.**

Give each person a clump of different-color clay. Say: **Shape your clay into a sculpture of yourself.**

After kids each have created a clay shape, have them each explain their shape. Commend kids on their creativity and uniqueness. Then have kids all squish their clay together into one big clump. Keep squishing the clay until each shape is indistinguishable. Then ask:

● **What happened to your shape?**

Say: **All the shapes got squished together so we can't tell one from another. That's like what happens when you try to act like everyone else. You hide what makes you special. God made you unique. There's no one else exactly like you. As a Christian, God wants you to act like the person he made you to be.**

4 Windsocks

(You'll need neon-color posterboard, tempera paint, paint brushes, glitter, sequins, construction paper, glue, scissors, staples and a stapler, streamers, sturdy string and a fan.)

Say: **You're a unique person created by God. He made you just the way you are so you'll be special to him and to others. To close, we're going to make windsocks that represent our uniqueness.**

Give kids the supplies you've collected. From the posterboard, have kids each cut a rectangle about 2 feet long and 1 foot wide. Staple each posterboard rectangle with the long ends together so it forms a tube. See the illustration below. Have kids each decorate their posterboard tube with the other supplies. Encourage kids to express their own uniqueness when decorating their windsocks.

When kids are finished decorating, have kids staple streamers to one end of the tube. Then staple both ends of a 1-foot string to the other end of the tube so kids can hang their windsocks.

Have kids hold their windsocks in the air. Turn a fan on the windsocks, and explain how the windsocks blowing in the wind are like the way God shows himself uniquely through each person.

Ask your senior pastor to let your kids hang their windsocks in your church foyer for all church members to see.

Windsock

5 | Mixed ice cream

(For each person, you'll need a bowl of vanilla ice cream, a spoon and a handful of M&M's.)

Give kids each a bowl of vanilla ice cream, a handful of M&M's and a spoon. Have kids mix the M&M's into their ice cream.

Say: **Just as the candy mixes with the ice cream yet still maintains its shape, you too can mix with your friends and still be special and unique.**

Let kids enjoy their ice cream.

The Big, Bad Pressure Zone

How many times have you bought a pair of pants or a dress just because it was "in"? Or changed your hairstyle to fall in line with current trends—even if you didn't like the current trends?

That many, huh? Well, you're not alone.

Peer pressure plagues just about every age group. We all feel the nagging push to look, act and even smell like everyone else. Often, this pressure can be relatively harmless. After all, no one ever died from a wild hairstyle (except Absalom!). But some pressures can cause far more damage if given the chance.

The elementary years are a good time to help kids learn to deal with negative peer pressure. Kids have already experienced the desire to be like everyone else, and kids are already being exposed to the dangers of drugs, pornography, premarital sex and a rebellious lifestyle. For this reason, it's important to teach kids how to say no.

Objectives

In this meeting, elementary kids will:
- learn the difference between good and bad peer pressure;
- understand the results of bad peer pressure;
- receive Christ's power to say no to bad peer pressure; and
- decide to exert the right kind of influence on friends.

The Meeting

1 To do or not to do

(You'll need Bibles and paper. Photocopy and cut apart the "Crazy Pressure" instructions on page 85.

by
Esther M. Bailey

Make enough copies so each person can have one instruction.)

Give kids each a "Crazy Pressure" instruction. It's okay if more than one person has the same instruction. Tell kids they each may carry out the instruction or simply read aloud what's written and tell why they won't do it.

After kids each have had a chance to read their instruction and make a choice, call everyone together. Have kids who didn't follow their instructions read them aloud and explain why they chose not to follow them. Then ask:

● **What made some of these instructions good and some bad?**

● **Why should we avoid bad or destructive activities?**

● **What would you do if someone you like told you to do something harmful to yourself or someone else?**

Say: **Others can pressure us to do good or bad. Your parents pressure you to do your homework; that's good pressure. But a classmate at school might pressure you to look at dirty magazines; that's bad pressure. We need to learn how to say no to bad pressure.**

2 Scripture pressure

(You'll need a Bible.)

Say: **Let's see what the Bible tells us about saying no to bad pressure. Maybe we can find something to help us do what's right when our friends are doing wrong.**

Have kids who read the scriptures in the first activity read them again—this time aloud. If your kids aren't comfortable reading aloud, read the passages yourself.

After someone reads Proverbs 22:24-25, ask:

● **What happens when we make friends with hot-tempered people?**

● **What other kinds of people should we not hang around with?**

● **Should never talk to them? Why or why not?**

Say: **We should avoid hanging around with people who pressure us to do bad things, such as getting angry a lot. That doesn't mean we shouldn't ever talk to them or be nice to them. We need to treat them with kindness like Jesus would. But we shouldn't spend all our time with them.**

After someone reads 1 Corinthians 5:9-11, ask:

● **Why should we avoid people who pretend to be Christians but don't really act like it?**

Say: **If we hang around people who only pretend to be Christians but really aren't, they might influence us to do things Christians shouldn't do.**

After someone reads 3 John 11, ask:

● **What kinds of people should be your friends?**

Say: **One of the best ways to say no to bad pressure is to avoid being around people who pressure you to do bad things.**

3 The power to choose

(You'll need an outdoor location near a large boulder, pole or tree.)

Take kids outside to a large boulder, pole or tree that a child can easily get a grip on. Have a volunteer stand in front of the group. Tell the volunteer to choose a spot on the grass and to remain there no matter what.

Have another volunteer pull the first person off his or her spot. Ask:

● **Why couldn't the first person stay on the spot?**

Say: **Sometimes even when you make a decision about something, others can pressure you to go against your decision whether you like it or not. Sometimes the pressure is too strong to fight. In the same way, even when we choose to do good things, bad pressures can come and push us into doing something bad. Sometimes we don't have enough strength to say no.**

Ask:

● **What do we need to make us strong?**

Have the volunteer wrap his or her arms around the tree, pole or boulder and hold on tightly. Have another volunteer try to pull the first volunteer from his or her spot. After a few tries, have the volunteers sit down.

Say: **We need to hold on to something to help us stand our ground. In the same way, we need Jesus' power to help us do what's right even when the pressure to do wrong is really strong.**

Ask:

● **How do we get Jesus' power to help us say no to bad pressures?**

Say: **Jesus will help us if we'll just ask him and if we're willing to do our best to act like him every day. Jesus wants to help us say no to bad pressure.**

4 Pressure review

(For each group of two or three, you'll need a photocopy of the "Pressure Time" handout on page 86 and a pencil.)

Form groups of two or three. Give groups each a "Pressure Time" handout and a pencil. Have groups each complete the handout. Circulate and encourage kids to think about the situations presented in the handout.

When groups are finished, call everyone together and have kids explain their answers. Ask:

● **Was it hard to tell what was right in these situations? Why or why not?**

● **What will you do if you're ever faced with a situation similar to one of these?**

Say: **Another way to say no to bad pressure is to decide what you will and won't do long before you're ever pressured to do the wrong thing.**

5 Pressure pact

(For each person, you'll need a 3×5 card and a pencil.)

Form a circle. Give kids each a 3×5 card and a pencil. On one side of their card, have kids each write this open-ended pledge: "I will never allow anyone to pressure me to . . . "

Have kids each complete the pledge with a bad pressure, such as drink, take drugs, have sex, smoke, cheat or tell lies. Explain that kids won't have to reveal what they've written.

On the other side of their card, have kids each write this open-ended pledge: "I will try to influence others to do good by . . . "

Have kids each complete this pledge with a good pressure, such as asking friends to church, praying for others or helping friends with homework.

When everyone's finished, have volunteers share what they wrote for the second pledge. Ask kids each to hold their pledge card over their heart as you pray: **Dear Jesus, when you were here on Earth, you didn't go along with the bad things others were doing. Help us also say no to those who want us to do bad things. Give us courage and power to always do what's right. In your name, amen.**

6 Pressure snack

(For each person, you'll need cookies and a canned soft drink.)

Serve cookies and canned soft drinks. As kids open their soft-drink cans, say: **When you open your soft-drink can, the pressure inside gushes out and is released. In the same way, when you ask Jesus to help you say no to bad pressure, he opens a way for the pressure to "gush" out of our lives. And we're free to do what's right.**

Crazy Pressure

Instructions: Photocopy and cut apart these instructions to use in activity 1. Make enough copies so each person can have one situation.

- ✂ - - - -

Sing "Happy Birthday" to the person whose birthday is closest to today.

- ✂ - - - -

Make a paper airplane and sail it through the air.

- ✂ - - - -

Read Proverbs 22:24-25.

- ✂ - - - -

Go home and cut up all your clothes.

- ✂ - - - -

Go jump in a lake.

- ✂ - - - -

Read 1 Corinthians 5:9-11.

- ✂ - - - -

Give someone all your money.

- ✂ - - - -

Try to persuade someone to drink a beer with you.

- ✂ - - - -

Compliment someone on what he or she is wearing.

- ✂ - - - -

Read 3 John 11.

- ✂ - - - -

Stand in front of the group and make silly faces.

- ✂ - - - -

PRESSURE TIME

Instructions: Circle what your group thinks is the best response for each situation below.

1. Margaret promised to babysit her two younger brothers on Saturday while her mother goes shopping. At the last minute Margaret gets a chance to go swimming with her friends. Margaret's mother says she'll take the younger kids with her even though it'll make shopping hard for her. Margaret should:
   (a) go with her friends.
   (b) take her brothers with her to the pool.
   (c) stay home and babysit.

2. When two junior high friends try to persuade Greg to take a puff on a cigarette, he should:
   (a) say, "No thanks, I'm trying to cut down."
   (b) try one.
   (c) preach a sermon about the evils of tobacco.

3. During recess several of Dianna's friends gather around to look at a magazine. When Dianna enters the room, someone says, "Oh, Dianna. You have to see this." A quick glance at the magazine tells Dianna it isn't something a Christian should look at. She should:
   (a) pretend to be slightly interested, then sneak away.
   (b) politely but firmly announce she doesn't want to look at the magazine.
   (c) tell her friends what terrible sinners they are to be looking at such a magazine.

4. Three of Jim's friends ask him to go for a hike in the woods. When they're alone, one of the boys brings out a little package of pills. "I got these from my brother," he says. "I tried one and it was a great feeling. Now we can all find out what a 'high' is like." The other two boys take the pills. Jim should:
   (a) accept the pill and pretend to take it.
   (b) take the pill, figuring that one time won't hurt him.
   (c) say, "You'll have to count me out on this one, guys."

5. When Michael, a popular seventh-grade boy, shows interest in Nancy, she's flattered. Then Michael plans a party and invites Nancy. Nancy knows his reputation for making out with girls. One of Nancy's friends, Chris, is also invited, but Chris' mother won't let her go unless Nancy goes. Chris begs Nancy to go. Nancy should:
   (a) tell the boy she can't go.
   (b) go because Chris wants her to.
   (c) go because she likes Michael.

Getting Along

Elementary children are uncoordinated socially. Some kids are shy. Some are boisterous. And many are self-conscious. Few know how to reach out and *really* get to know people.

Elementary kids need to learn how to get along with others and accept people who are different, says Jim Lochner, a professor of health, physical education and recreation at Weber State College in Ogden, Utah. And learning to get along with others is easier once kids learn some basic relationship skills.

Objectives

In this meeting, elementary kids will:
- pair up with different kids in the group and ask personal questions;
- write qualities they admire in others;
- identify people in the Bible who got along with each other; and
- choose one quality to work on to be a better person.

The Meeting

1 Stop and ask

(You'll need a whistle. For each person, you'll need a photocopy of the "Questions Quiz" handout on page 91.)

As children arrive, give them each a "Questions Quiz" handout. Explain that kids each will pair up with someone in the room and ask one question from the handout. Then when they hear the whistle, have kids each switch partners and ask a different question of their new partner.

To start the activity, blow the whistle, signaling kids each to find a partner. After 15 to 30 seconds, blow the whistle again. Blow the whistle a total of 10 times so kids can ask all 10 ques-

by
**Jolene L.
Roehlkepartain**

tions and mingle with 10 different kids. If you have fewer than 10 kids, allow them to pair up with the same person more than once.

After the activity, ask:

● **Did you learn anything new about the people you talked to? Why or why not?**

● **How do questions help you get to know people?**

● **Where else could you use these questions?**

Say: **You could use these questions to get to know people at school, at church or anywhere you find people. Asking questions can help us get along with others, because the more we know about people, the more we're able to see how special God thinks they are.**

2 Star qualities

(For each person, you'll need a marker, scissors, a sheet of yellow construction paper and some tape.)

Give kids each a marker, scissors and a sheet of yellow construction paper. Have kids each draw and cut out a full-page star. Then have kids help each other tape their stars to their backs.

Say: **To God, each of you shines brightly and beautifully like a star. We should recognize the star qualities in each other. On each person's star, write something you admire about him or her.**

When everyone is finished, have kids each remove their star and read what others wrote. Remind kids that people everywhere are special to God, even if they're not just like us.

3 Get-along hopscotch

(For each pair, you'll need two buttons, a photocopy of the "Bible Hopscotch" handout on page 92, and a set of photocopied, cut-apart "Bible Pairs" slips on page 93.)

Form pairs. Give each pair two buttons, a "Bible Hopscotch" handout and a set of "Bible Pairs" slips.

Before the game, say: **Many people in the Bible got along with others—even if they were different. In this game, you'll identify people who got along with someone else.**

Your buttons are your game pieces. Draw a slip and read it

aloud—except for the answer. If your partner correctly identifies the missing person, move your partner's button one space on the hopscotch board. If your partner guesses incorrectly, don't move the button.

Take turns until all the slips have been used. The person whose button makes it the farthest on the hopscotch board is the winner.

After pairs are finished, call everyone together and congratulate the winners. Say: **These Bible partners learned to get along with each other, even though they were each different in some way. As Christians, we need to learn to get along with others too—whether they're just like us or not.**

Ask:

● **What are ways people might be different from you?**

● **Why is it good to get to know people who are different?**

● **What's one way you can try to get to know someone who's different from you?**

Say: **There are lots of qualities we can use to help us get along with others. Let's find out what some of them are.**

4 The Bible says

(You'll need three Bibles, three packages of 3×5 cards and three markers. You'll also need smiley-face stickers for one-third of your group. On a sheet of newsprint, write these references: Proverbs 12:22; Malachi 2:6; Matthew 5:1-10; Galatians 5:22-23; Galatians 6:10; Ephesians 5:9; Philippians 2:3-4; and Colossians 3:13-14. Tape the newsprint to a wall.)

Form three teams. A team can be one person. Give each team a Bible, a package of 3×5 cards and a marker. Give teams five minutes to look up the Bible passages on the newsprint and identify qualities they need to get along with people. Teams each must write each quality on a separate card, and try to identify as many different qualities as they can.

After five minutes, ask teams each to total the number of qualities they found. Award smiley-face stickers to the team with the most qualities.

Call everyone together and read aloud what kids wrote on their cards. Commend kids on their thorough work.

5 Friends stick together

(For each person, you'll need a sheet of construction paper, glue and glitter.)

Say: **Now that we've found a lot of different "getting along" qualities in the Bible, choose one quality you'd like to work on to be a better friend.**

Give kids each a sheet of construction paper, glue and some glitter. Have kids each write their chosen quality with glue on their construction paper and then sprinkle the glue with glitter. Say: **Friends need to stick together. Over the next week, work on this quality to make your relationships sparkle. Take your word home with you and hang it on your bedroom door as a reminder to work on being a better friend.**

6 Take time

(For each person, you'll need a photocopy of the "Take Time" handout on page 94 and a marker. For each person, you'll also need a "get along" snack, such as Oreo cookies and milk, or a peanut butter and jelly sandwich.)

Give kids each a "Take Time" handout and a marker. Say: **To be good friends, we have to take time out to be with people. With your marker, write on the clock different times you should take time to be a good friend.**

Kids could write "when someone is sad," "when someone is hurting" or "when someone has exciting news." When everyone is finished, have kids form a circle and join hands.

Close with this prayer: **Thank you, God, for helping us get along with others. Help us take time to get to know others and be a friend. In Jesus' name, amen.**

After the prayer, treat kids to snacks that "get along" well together, such as Oreo cookies and milk, or peanut butter and jelly sandwiches.

QUESTIONS QUIZ

Instructions: Find a different partner to ask each of these questions.

1. What's your favorite color? Why?

2. Which household chore do you dislike most? Why?

3. What's your favorite subject in school? Why?

4. What's your favorite season of the year? Why?

5. What's your favorite Bible verse? Why?

6. If you had $20 to spend, how would you spend it? Why?

7. What bores you most? Why?

8. Which Bible character do you like most? Why?

9. What do you most enjoy doing in your free time? Why?

10. If you could solve one of the world's problems, which one would you solve? Why?

Bible Hopscotch

Instructions: Use this hopscotch board to keep track of how many missing-person identities you guess correctly.

Place Bible-pair slips here.

Bible Pairs

Instructions: For every two kids in your group, photocopy a set of these Bible pairs. Then cut them apart and put the slips into a pile.

Adam and _____(Eve)

Ruth and_____(Naomi or Boaz)

Elizabeth and_____(Zechariah)

Mary and _____(Joseph)

Moses and _____(Aaron)

Rachel and_____(Leah or Jacob)

Isaac and _____(Jacob or Rebekah)

Paul and _____(Barnabas or Silas)

James and _____(John)

Abraham and _____(Sarah)

Jonathan and _____(David)

Martha and_____(Mary)

TAKE TIME

Instructions: On the clock, write different ways you can be a good friend.

Part 4
My World

We're One Small Corner

Courtney Walsh, a young person from Memphis, Tennessee, wanted to discover what the world was really like. But she didn't have a way to travel around the world and make friends with people in different countries. So instead of traveling, she started writing letters to kids all over the world.

Courtney found a way to see the world without ever leaving her bedroom. She looks through her pen pals' eyes. She now has 200 pen pals who live in 18 countries.

Just like adults, children get caught up in their own lives. Without meaning to, they often become unaware of how other people live. Use this meeting to help children experience what other children go through every day.

Objectives

In this meeting, elementary kids will:
- experience how people in different countries live;
- discuss how they can help others in need;
- apply the good Samaritan story to their lives; and
- celebrate God's love for all people everywhere.

The Meeting

1 Assign a country

(You'll need a large open room. With masking tape, divide the room into four sections, or "countries." Write these "country" names on separate sheets of posterboard: Richland, Underland, Industrous and Populous. Place each posterboard in a different country section. Use the "Country Guide" on page 98 to help you prepare each country. You'll need a hat, and for each person you'll need a slip of paper and a pencil.)

by
Kelli Woodall

Country Guide

Instructions: Set up each country according to the guidelines below.

Richland

Room—Provide a chair for each person.

Supplies—Set out a 2-foot dowel rod, poster-board, a full package of different-color construction paper, scissors, glue, glitter, a stapler and different-color markers.

Snack—Set out a full pitcher of lemonade, a full pitcher of ice, a large spoon, cups, napkins and several types of cookies.

Underland

Room—Provide nothing.

Supplies—Provide none.

Snack—Set out two stalks of celery and a cup of powdered lemonade mix. Don't provide any water.

Populous

Room—Provide chairs for half the group.

Supplies—Provide a few sheets of construction paper and a marker.

Snack—Set out a few crackers, one glass of lemonade and a few napkins.

Industrous

Room—Provide a table for kids to sit on.

Supplies—Provide one sheet of black construction paper, some different-color markers, glue and glitter.

Snack—Set out one cracker and a glass of lemonade for each person.

Give kids each a slip of paper and a pencil. Have kids each write their name on their paper. Collect the names, and place them in a hat. Draw names from the hat and randomly assign children to their countries. Make sure Populous gets more children than the others. Tell kids that once they enter their country they may not go into another country.

After kids have entered their countries, give them a few minutes to get settled. Remind kids they may not enter another country or remove any objects from their country. Say: **Today we're going to talk about what it's like to live in different kinds of countries. Each of you is now a citizen of the country you're in. Let's see what we can discover about each of these strange lands.**

2 Richland winners

(You'll need the supplies for each country. See the "Country Guide" on page 98.)

Have a flag-making contest. Groups may each use only supplies found in their own country. When everyone's finished, have each group present its flag. Award Richland first place, even if its flag isn't the best.

Say: **Richland can make a better flag because the citizens are rich. They have more supplies than other countries.**

Have countries each display their flag where others can see it.

Say: **Now let's have a scavenger hunt to see which country comes out on top.**

Have countries each choose a runner. Explain that you'll call out an item, such as a watch or a brush. Each country's citizens will look for that item and, if they have it, give it to their runner. The runner will then bring it to you. The first country to get the item to you gets 1 point. Play until one country gets 10 points. Start by naming items available in all countries, such as lemonade, a shoe or a button. As you continue to play, call out more and more items available only to Richland, such as a large spoon or a cookie. Make sure Richland wins.

After the game, ask:
● **Was this game fair? Why or why not?**
● **What would make the game more fair?**

Say: **Richland won because it has more supplies than any other country. One way we could make the game more fair is to have Richland give some of its supplies away to the other countries. It's like that in the real world too. People who have** a lot should give some of what they have to people who have only a little. That way everyone's needs can be met. But it doesn't always happen that way.

3 Some go hungry

(You'll need the refreshments you prepared for each country. See the "Country Guide" on page 98.)

Serve refreshments. Allow kids to share food if they want to, but don't suggest it. Say: **Some of you don't have much to eat for a snack. It's like that in the real world too. In many countries, not everybody gets enough to eat.**

Ask:

● **What should we do to help hungry people around the world?**

● **What can you do to help others who don't have enough to eat?**

Say: **We shouldn't act selfish and keep all the good things we have to ourselves. We need to learn to help others who truly need it.**

4 Country questions

(No supplies needed.)

Have kids leave their countries and form a circle.

Ask:

● **Did you like your country? Why or why not?**

● **Which country did you like best? Explain.**

● **How could your country have helped Underland? Populous?**

● **How are our countries like real-world countries?**

Say: **Countries in the real world are different from each other—just like ours are different. Some countries are rich, others have no money. Some have too many people. Some are full of factories and businesses that make lots of money. Not all the countries are equal. But we should do all we can to help others who have needs—whether they're in other countries or right next door.**

5 | Who's my neighbor?

(You'll need a Bible and a photocopy of the "Good Country" handout on page 102.)

Have kids return to their countries. Read aloud Luke 10:30-34. Say: **This story tells us we should help others when we can. Let's act out this story, but let's change it to fit our countries.**

Choose a volunteer from each country to act out the "Good Country" story. Say to the actors: **I'll read the story and tell you what to do as we go.**

Clear a space in the center of the room and have all the actors stand to one side. Read aloud the "Good Country" story, directing actors as needed.

After the story, commend actors for their efforts. Then ask:

● **Which of the three countries did the right thing for the man from Populous?**

● **What can we do to help the people around us like the man from Underland helped the man from Populous?**

Say: **People all over the world have needs. But there are people around us every day who also need our help. You can be like the man from Underland by making friends with kids who seem lonely or by inviting a friend to church. And you can pray for people too. That's one of the best ways to help others.**

6 | World snacks

(For each person, you'll need an international treat, such as a sopapilla or a French pastry.)

Have kids leave their countries again and sit in a circle in the center of the room. Say: **God loves the people who live in all the countries of the world. Let's celebrate different countries by eating special treats from different lands. While I pass out these treats, let's sing "Jesus Loves the Little Children."**

Give kids each an international treat, and lead them in singing "Jesus Loves the Little Children." As kids enjoy their treats, tell about the country the treats came from.

When everyone's finished, close with prayer. Thank God for all the countries in the world and ask him to teach kids to help others who have needs.

Good Country

Instructions: Read aloud this story, instructing actors as directed in the text. The story is based on Luke 10:30-34.

A man from Populous was going down from Jerusalem to Jericho. (Have the Populous actor walk to the center of the room.) **As he went, he was attacked by robbers. They stripped his clothes, beat him and went away, leaving him half dead.** (Have the Populous actor fall down and act hurt.)

A man from Richland happened to be going down the same road. (Have the Richland actor walk up to the Populous actor.) **And when he saw the man from Populous, he passed by quickly without helping him.** (Have the Richland actor walk by quickly.)

Then a man from Industrous walked by. (Have the Industrous actor come up to the Populous actor.) **When he saw the man from Populous, he also walked by quickly without helping him.** (Have the Industrous actor walk by quickly.)

Finally a man from Underland came by and happened to see the man. (Have the Underland actor walk up to the Populous actor.) **The man from Underland felt sorry for the man from Populous. He bandaged his wounds.** (Have the Underland actor pretend to bandage the Populous man's wounds.) **Then the man from Underland took the man from Populous to an inn and helped him get well.** (Have the Underland actor pull the Populous actor to the side of the room and help him stand up.)

The end.

Drugs and Drinking

I t's hard to accept, but elementary-age kids are drinking and taking drugs. They think it's fun.

Instead of looking to dangerous substances to find fun and fulfillment, kids need to see the wonderful gifts God has given them for their enjoyment. Seeing the truth—that using alcohol and drugs has negative consequences, and that using God's gifts has positive consequences—will help them make the right choices.

This lesson will help kids learn to celebrate God's gifts and avoid alcohol and drugs.

Objectives

In this meeting, elementary kids will:
● learn about God's gifts;
● discover the consequences of drinking and taking drugs;
● think of ways to enjoy God's gifts; and
● ask God to help them say no to drugs and alcohol.

The Meeting

1 God's gifts

(For each person, you'll need a pencil and a photocopy of the "God's Gifts" handout on page 107.)

If possible, take kids outside for the first part of this meeting. Give kids each a "God's Gifts" handout and a pencil. Have kids search for the items on the handout and draw what they find.

Then form a circle and have kids each share their completed handout with the group. Ask:
● **What did you discover about God's gifts?**

by
Christine Yount

● **How can we enjoy God's gifts each day?**

● **What are other gifts God has given us?**

Say: **God has given us many gifts. And we can enjoy those gifts every day. But some things in the world should be avoided. Two of those things are drugs and alcohol. You've probably seen people drinking or taking drugs on TV shows or in movies. They may seem like fun things to try, but they can be dangerous.**

2 Forbidden fruit

(You'll need a Bible. For each person, you'll need a piece of fruit, such as an apple or peach.)

Read aloud Genesis 3:1-11. Ask:

● **What gifts did God give Adam and Eve?**

● **What did Adam and Eve do that God told them not to do?**

● **What happened after Adam and Eve made a bad choice?**

Say: **Adam and Eve made a bad decision when they chose to eat the fruit of the tree of knowledge. Many people today make bad choices too, especially when it comes to drugs and alcohol. And, just as Adam and Eve had to deal with the consequences of their bad choice, we have to deal with the consequences when we make bad choices.**

Give kids each a piece of fruit. Form a circle and begin passing the fruit clockwise around the circle. Tell kids to be careful not to drop the fruit. After a few seconds, drop a piece of fruit to the ground so it bruises. Then keep passing the rest of the fruit around the circle. After another minute, call time and have kids each hold a piece of fruit. Give your piece of fruit to the person who is without one. Then pick up the bruised fruit and show it to the kids in the circle.

Say: **I made a bad choice when I dropped the fruit on the ground, and now it's bruised. When we choose to take drugs or alcohol, we may hurt ourselves just as I hurt this fruit.**

Ask:

● **What bad things might happen if you drink alcohol or take drugs?**

Say: **When we avoid drugs and alcohol, we can feel good about ourselves.**

Have kids each wash their piece of fruit and eat it.

3 Can prep

(You'll need a Bible, some empty soft-drink cans and some cans of light-color, quick drying spray paint. Set up an area in the room or outside where kids can spray paint their cans. Cover the floor or ground with newspapers or old sheets. And be sure you have plenty of ventilation in the area.)

Read aloud Philippians 4:13. Say: **With Jesus' help, we can stay away from alcohol and drugs. Let's each create a personal "can" to tell how we "can" stay away from drugs and alcohol.**

Give kids each an empty soft-drink can. Help kids each spray their can with a light-color, quick-drying paint. While kids are waiting for the paint to dry, go on to the next activity.

Say: **We'll come back to finish these in a few minutes.**

4 Alternative freeze tag

(No supplies needed.)

Say: **Sometimes, people drink or take drugs because they're bored and it seems like a fun thing to do. But there are many other things you can do instead that aren't dangerous. Think about things you can do instead of drinking or taking drugs. During this next game, we'll call out those ideas.**

Choose one person to be "It." "It" will run around and try to tag other kids. Tell kids they must freeze if they're tagged by "It." They may be unfrozen only if a friend tags them and calls out something kids can do instead of drinking or taking drugs. For example, someone might tag a person who's frozen and call out "Go to a movie," "Read a book" or "Play kickball with friends."

After a minute or two, ask for another volunteer to be "It." Play the game for about six minutes. Then ask:

● **What are some of the things people thought of to do instead of drinking or taking drugs?**

● **What could you say to someone who wants you to drink or take drugs?**

5 I can

(For each person, you'll need a marker.)

Give each child a marker. Have them each decorate their can with positive messages describing alternatives to drugs and alcohol. Remind kids to use the ideas called out during the Alternative Freeze Tag game. Kids might write "Reading is better than drinking" or "Try sports, not drugs" on their cans.

Form a circle and have kids hold up their decorated cans. Read aloud Philippians 4:13 again. In unison, have kids say, "I can stay away from drugs and alcohol."

6 God can

Have kids each place their can in the center of the circle. Then have kids hold hands. Close by saying the following prayer. Read it one line at a time and have kids repeat it after you:

Dear God, thank you for your gifts.
Thank you for good and fun things.
Help us enjoy your creation.
Help us say no to alcohol and drugs.
Amen.

Encourage kids to take their decorated cans home as reminders that they "can" say no to drugs and alcohol.

God's Gifts

Instructions: God has given us many gifts, including the warmth of the sun and the beauty of the flowers. Take a couple of minutes to look around and see God's gifts. Then look at the boxes below. Find at least one of God's gifts that fits the description in each box and draw a picture of it. For example, in the "Something big" box you might draw a tree or a mountain.

Something soft

Something smooth

Something shiny

Something green

Something tiny

Something that smells good

Something big

Feeling Good About School

According to a study by Weekly Reader, most second- and third-graders enjoy school. But once kids reach fourth grade, their enthusiasm for school drops significantly. Children's feelings toward school vary. Some elementary kids may feel bored with school. For others, certain subjects become less appealing than others. And some kids even begin to measure their self-esteem by how well they do in school.

By grappling with their feelings about school, kids can learn the importance of taking school seriously. And they can avoid lax study habits that may hinder them as they grow older.

Objectives

In this meeting, elementary kids will:
- identify what they like and dislike about school;
- give advice to help peers in school;
- see how their faith can help them at school; and
- affirm what they like about each other.

The Meeting

1 Lunch-bag mingle

(You'll need a whistle. For each person, you'll need a lunch bag with the following items in it: a pencil, an eraser, a sheet of paper and a piece of chalk.)

Give kids each a lunch bag as they arrive. To begin the game, tell kids that when you blow the whistle, they must each pull out one item from their bag and run to find other kids in the room who've pulled out the same item. When groups have formed, tell kids they'll take turns answering the questions you ask. Then they'll put their items back into their bags

by
**Jolene L.
Roehlkepartain**

and do the activity again—a total of four times.

Ask a different one of these questions each time:
- **What do you like most about school?**
- **What do you like least about school?**
- **What's good about being a Christian at school?**
- **What subject do you like best?**

After you ask all the questions, say: **Today we're going to talk about our feelings about school and how Jesus can help us feel good about school. Let's start by doing an activity you've probably done in school.**

2 | School word-search

(For each person, you'll need a photocopy of the "School Word-Search" handout on page 113 and a marker.)

Give kids each a marker and a "School Word-Search" handout. Have kids each follow the instructions and complete the word-search as quickly as possible. If kids need help finding particular words, refer to the completed "School Word-Search" below.

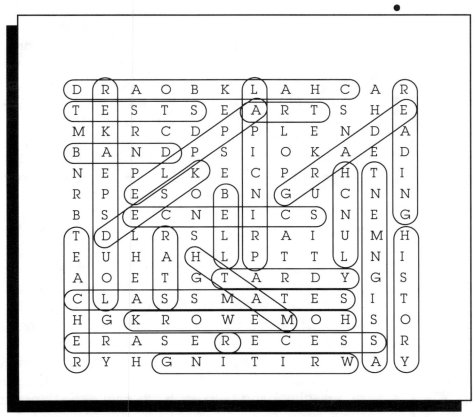

After a minute or two, call time. Ask:

● **How'd you feel as you rushed to complete the word-search?**

● **How is this activity like a typical day at school?**

Read aloud Colossians 3:23. Ask:

● **What does it mean to do your best work in all you do?**

● **How does this verse apply to schoolwork?**

● **Is it easy to do your best work when you feel rushed at school? Explain.**

Say: **From hearing announcements over the loudspeaker to visiting the principal to studying for a spelling test, a lot of different events fill each day at school. Just as you raced to search for the words on this word-search, you race to complete assignments, tests and other activities at school.**

You may look forward to certain activities while you dread others. This next activity will help you identify what you like and dislike about certain subjects at school.

3 Subject to discussion

(You'll need tape, newsprint and red, black and blue markers. Write each of the following school "subject" stations on a separate sheet of newsprint: recess, lunch, math, social studies, science and art. Tape the sheets of newsprint to the walls around your meeting room.)

Form three teams. Give one team red markers, another team black markers and the third team blue markers. Tell teams they must each write on the newsprint one thing they like about that subject and one thing they don't like about that subject. For example, kids might write, "Lunch is fun because you get to be with friends; lunch is hard because the food tastes bad."

Have the red team start at the recess station. Have the blue team start at the math station. Have the black team start at the art station. Give kids one minute to talk about the subject and write their comments on that sheet of newsprint. Then blow the whistle and have teams each rotate clockwise one station. Continue the exercise until teams each have written their comments on all six sheets of newsprint. Then have kids walk around the room and read what other teams wrote.

Say: **As you can see, we don't always agree on what we like or don't like about school. We can celebrate the things we like about school and help each other with the things we don't like.**

4 Advice box

(You'll need an empty shoe box. For each person, you'll need a 3×5 card and a marker.)

Have kids sit in a circle. Give each person a 3×5 card and a marker. Ask kids each to write on their card one thing they're struggling with at school and would like some advice about. Tell kids not to write their names on the cards.

After kids each have filled out their card, pass around an empty shoe box for kids to put their card in.

Have volunteers each pull out one card, read the problem aloud and then give their advice about the problem. If volunteers can't think of any advice, they can ask others for help.

Then have volunteers each hand the box to the person on their left. Continue around the circle until everyone has given advice.

5 School race

(You'll need a Bible. For each person, you'll need a photocopy of the "School Race" handout on page 114 and a marker.)

Read aloud 1 Corinthians 9:24-25. Ask:

● **How is going to school like running a race?**

Give kids each a "School Race" handout and a marker. Have kids each complete their handout. Then form pairs and have partners each read their completed handout.

6 Musical apples

(You'll need an apple, a cassette player and a cassette for background music.)

Say: **Just as our friends can help us deal with problems at school, they can help us feel good about who we are at school.**

Have kids stand in a circle. Give one person an apple. Explain that while the music plays, kids should pass the apple around the circle. When you stop the music, the person holding the apple must step inside the circle. The other kids must each then say something positive about the person in the center of the circle. Have kids say positive things relating to school. For example, kids may say, "I like how you always smile at school" or "You're really good at math."

After kids in the circle have each said something positive, the person in the middle must rejoin the circle and start passing the apple when the music starts. If kids who've already been in the center end up with the apple, they must give it to someone who hasn't. Play the game until each person has stood in the center of the circle.

7 Good apples

(You'll need one apple for each person.)

Give kids each one apple. As you give each child an apple, say: **You can succeed at school.** Then have kids form a circle and hold their apples toward the center of the circle until all the apples are touching. Have kids close their eyes.

Pray: **Thank you, God, for making us each special. Help us honestly deal with our feelings about school so we can be the best students we can be. Amen.**

Tell kids they can eat their apples.

SCHOOL WORD-SEARCH

Instructions: Find and circle the following words in this puzzle. Words may be forward, backward, horizontal, vertical or diagonal.

Look for: apple, art, assignment, band, bell, chalkboard, classmates, desk, eraser, grade, history, homework, loudspeaker, lunch, math, principal, reading, recess, science, star, tardy, teacher, tests, writing.

```
D  R  A  O  B  K  L  A  H  C  A  R
T  E  S  T  S  E  A  R  T  S  H  E
M  K  R  C  D  P  P  L  E  N  D  A
B  A  N  D  P  S  I  O  K  A  E  D
N  E  P  L  K  E  C  P  R  H  T  I
R  P  E  S  O  B  N  G  U  C  N  N
B  S  E  C  N  E  I  C  S  N  E  G
T  D  L  R  S  L  R  A  I  U  M  H
E  U  H  A  H  L  P  T  T  L  N  I
A  O  E  T  G  T  A  R  D  Y  G  S
C  L  A  S  S  M  A  T  E  S  I  T
H  G  K  R  O  W  E  M  O  H  S  O
E  R  A  S  E  R  E  C  E  S  S  R
R  Y  H  G  N  I  T  I  R  W  A  Y
```

School Race

Instructions: Sometimes keeping up with schoolwork is like running a race. You go from one subject to the next and from one test to the next with few breaks between. You may feel exhausted by the end of a day.

But you don't have to run out of energy. You can stop and get refreshment along the way. Follow the runner below, and at each drink station read the scripture listed. Write one or two words that describe how that passage can help "energize" you for the rest of the "school race."

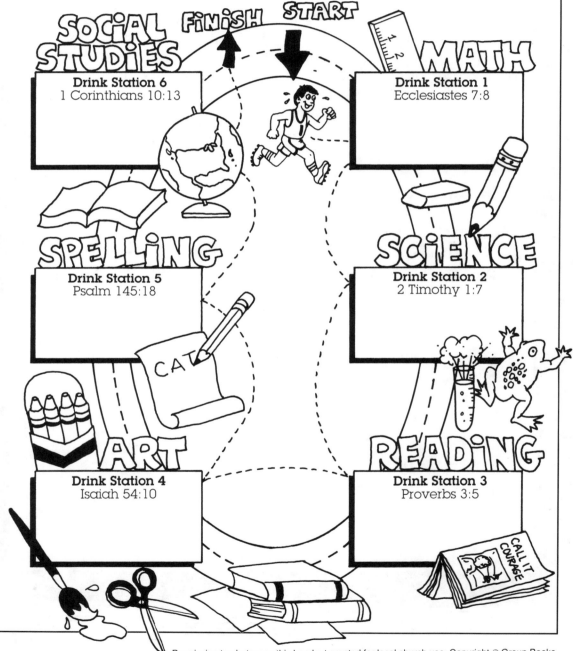

FINISH **START**

SOCIAL STUDIES
Drink Station 6
1 Corinthians 10:13

MATH
Drink Station 1
Ecclesiastes 7:8

SPELLING
Drink Station 5
Psalm 145:18

SCIENCE
Drink Station 2
2 Timothy 1:7

ART
Drink Station 4
Isaiah 54:10

READING
Drink Station 3
Proverbs 3:5

"I Want My Television!"

It's nearly impossible to count the ways television has influenced our daily lives. From fads to slang, television has made a major impact on our society.

Elementary children each average more than 20 hours a week in front of the TV set. During those hours, they're bound to see situations involving sex, alcohol abuse, bad language, violence and drugs.

The video and cable-TV boom has only added to the problem. Now children can see movies in their homes that would require an adult's presence to see in the movie theater.

In this meeting, kids will learn valuable decision-making skills and biblical principles to apply to TV-watching. But be warned, kids see you as a role model in this area. Don't expect them to change their TV habits without examining yours!

Objectives

In this meeting elementary kids will:
- identify several of their favorite TV shows;
- research and discuss Bible verses related to what they see and hear;
- think about how Jesus would react to the shows they watch; and
- write a TV schedule for God-honoring viewing habits.

The Meeting

1 TV scramble

(You'll need a large room. Tape sheets of newsprint to the wall. You'll need markers and bags of popcorn.) Form at least three teams, with no more than five kids to a

by
Rick Chromey

team. A team must be at least two people. To form teams, name a popular TV show and ask kids who watched it the previous week to raise their hands. If you need three per team, the first three to raise their hands will be a team. Name another popular program and create another team. Do this until everyone is on a team. The teams will each take on the name of the TV show.

Once teams have been formed, have kids begin to think about their favorite TV shows. Line teams up so each is several feet away from a sheet of newsprint. Give a marker to the first person on each team.

Say: **The object of this relay is to list as many TV shows as possible within two minutes. The first person on each team must run up to the newsprint and list one show. Then he or she must run to the end of the line and pass the marker up to the front for the next person to use. The team that lists the most shows within two minutes wins.**

After two minutes, call time. Give a bag of popcorn to each member of the winning team.

2 Wheel of principles

(You'll need Bibles, paper, pencils and tape.)

Have kids stay in their teams and sit in the middle of the room. Ask:

- **How many hours a day do you watch television?**
- **What are your favorite shows?**
- **What TV shows do you dislike the most?**
- **Who's your favorite TV character?**
- **Who's your least-favorite TV character?**

Say: **Whether we watch a lot of television or a little, it's a part of our lives. Today we're going to look at our viewing habits and talk about how the Bible can help us come up with guidelines for watching television.**

Give teams each a Bible, two sheets of paper, a pencil and one of the following scripture verses: Psalm 101:3; Psalm 119:37; Romans 12:2; and Philippians 4:8. If you have more than four teams, assign the same verse to more than one team. If you have fewer than four teams, assign more than one verse to each team.

Say: **We're going to play a game based on your scripture verses. In your group, look up and read your verse. Then talk about how it relates to watching television. On your paper,** write a short sentence that tells how the verse can apply to TV-watching. Make sure your sentence is no longer than seven words.

After teams each have a sentence, say: **Now use a new sheet of paper and draw a large box for each letter in your sentence as if you were creating a puzzle for Wheel of Fortune.**

Show kids the example below if they aren't sure what to do.

Sentence: We should avoid bad things.

Puzzle:

□□ □□□□□□
□□□□□ □□□ □□□□□□

Tape one team's puzzle to the wall, and have other teams sit where they can see it. Have a representative of the team that created the puzzle be your assistant as you play the game. The assistant should have a written-out copy of the sentence.

Have teams that didn't create the puzzle take turns guessing letters that might be in the puzzle. Keep track of the letters kids guess. When a team guesses a letter that's in the sentence, have your assistant write that letter in the puzzle wherever it appears. A team may guess letters until it guesses one that isn't in the puzzle, then the next team may guess.

A team may choose to guess the entire sentence during its turn. If the team gets it exactly right, that team wins the round. If the team guesses any words wrong, the next team gets to continue with its turn. Play until the sentence is guessed. Then play the other teams' puzzles in the same way.

When all the puzzles have been solved, read the sentences aloud. Ask:

● **How easy was it to solve the puzzles?**
● **What does the Bible say about watching television?**
● **What can we learn from the scriptures that can help us make good TV-watching decisions?**

Say: **It was hard to figure out these puzzles because we didn't know what the sentences said. In the same way, it's hard to figure out what to watch on television because sometimes we don't know what a show will be like.**

3 God in a box

Have teams each find a place in the room apart from the other teams.

Say: **Imagine for a moment that your team is just getting ready to watch television together. Talk among yourselves about what show you want to watch. Try to convince your team members that the show you want to watch is the best one. Be sure to say why you think it's the best. For this activity, pretend all the shows are on at the same time.**

Give kids one or two minutes to discuss the shows they'd like to watch. Then say: **You finally decide on a show. As you turn on your television, you hear a knock on the door. Standing outside your door is . . . Jesus!**

Ask:
● **What show were you watching?**
● **How would Jesus react to the show?**
● **Is this a show Jesus would feel okay about watching? Why or why not?**
● **What would embarrass you about watching the show with Jesus?**
● **What would make you feel good about watching the show with Jesus?**

4 TV guide

(For each person, you'll need a photocopy of the "TV Guide" handout on page 119 and a pencil.)

Give kids each a "TV Guide" handout and a pencil. Have kids each complete the handout, keeping in mind what they learned from the Bible during this meeting.

Ask volunteers to share what they've written.

Say: **Before you turn on the television, think about what's good and bad about the show you want to watch. Ask yourself what Jesus would think about the show. Then make your viewing decision.**

Form a circle and close in prayer, thanking God for the ability to choose carefully what we watch on television.

5 | Name-that-theme-song snack time

(Set cookies and punch on a table in the room. If possible, get a copy of the cassette or album *Television's Greatest Hits* or something similar, and a cassette player or record player.)

Before letting kids eat the snacks, have teams each sing a theme song to a popular TV show. Just for fun, sing the theme song of a show you like.

While kids are snacking, play the *Television's Greatest Hits* cassette or record. Have kids guess the TV shows belonging to the theme songs played.

TV GUIDE

"Keep me from looking at worthless things. Let me live by your word" (Psalm 119:37).

A TV show Jesus would watch with me: _____

A TV show Jesus probably wouldn't watch: _____

I'll be more careful in my TV-watching by doing the following things:

_____

_____

_____

_____

_____

_____

_____

_____

_____

_____

_____

I Love You Through Death

Death is an often-ignored subject among children. Many kids can't imagine dying soon. Others simply don't want to think about loss or tragedy in their lives. But recent rises in the teenage-suicide rate have focused more attention on death at an alarmingly young age. A USA Today poll lists the #1 worry of 72 percent of 5- to 16-year-olds as death of a parent. And 56 percent say they worry about dying themselves.

This lesson will help kids deal with their worries about death.

Objectives

In this meeting, elementary kids will:
● name fears associated with death;
● share feelings about the death of loved ones;
● recognize how death can affect their lives; and
● appreciate God's gift of eternal life for us.

The Meeting

1 Tombstone tags

(Cut gray construction paper into tombstone-shape name tags. You'll need markers and tape.)

As kids arrive, give them each a name tag and a marker. Have kids each write on their name tag their name and one thing they'd like said about them after they die. For example, kids might write, "He was a good singer" or "She was loved by everyone." Tell kids not to show their name tags to anyone else. When kids have finished writing their name tags, collect them.

by
Margaret
Hinchey

One at a time, read aloud what kids wrote on their name tags—except for their names. After reading each one, have kids guess who they think wrote what you just read. Remind kids each to "guess" other names when their description is read to fool other kids.

As name-tag owners are guessed correctly, have owners each tape their name tag to their clothes. Ask:

- **How easy was it to guess who wrote each name tag?**
- **Was it easy to think of something to write on your name tag?**

2 | Death fears

(For each person, you'll need a photocopy of the "Death Fears" handout on page 125 and a pencil.)

Say: **Today we're going to explore a difficult subject— death. Death isn't easy to talk about. But if you're like many other kids, you probably think about death sometimes. In Romans 6:23, we learn that "When someone sins, he earns what sin pays—death." That means that because of sin we'll all die sometime.**

But we don't know when we'll die. And we don't know when someone close to us—a parent, brother, sister or friend—will die. That can be a scary feeling. Today we're going to talk about the feelings we have about death.

Give kids each a "Death Fears" handout and a pencil. Ask kids each to complete the handout. Tell them they won't be asked to tell what they wrote.

When everyone's finished, ask:

- **How'd you feel as you completed your handout?**
- **Did you check exactly the same things in each column? Why or why not?**
- **Do you feel differently about your own death than about the death of others? Why or why not?**
- **What other words did you add to describe your feelings?**

Encourage kids to talk about how they feel about death. Ask:

- **How would things change if a parent or friend died tonight?**

3 Missing persons

(You'll need two sheets of paper and two pencils.)

Have kids line up along a wall in birthday order—from the earliest in the year to the latest.

Say: **Now let's have a birthday shout to see if everyone's in the right order.**

Beginning with the earliest birthday, have kids each shout out their birth date in order.

Determine the middle of the line, and form two groups by dividing the group at the middle. Have the early-in-the-year-birthday group go to one end of the room and the late-in-the-year-birthday group go to the other.

Have groups each determine who's the oldest in their group and have that person be their scribe. Give the scribe for each group a sheet of paper and a pencil.

Have the late-in-the-year-birthday group step out of the room. Go to the early-in-the-year-birthday group and say: **Imagine that everyone from the other group has vanished in a mysterious way and will never appear again.**

Go to the late-in-the-year-birthday group outside the room and say: **Imagine that everyone from the other group has vanished in a mysterious way and will never appear again.**

Tell groups each to brainstorm the things they'll miss about the people in the "missing" group. Say: **Imagine how things would be different if these people were really gone. But remember to keep your comments positive.**

Have scribes list the things people brainstorm. For example, someone's sense of humor or nice smile might be missed.

Allow five minutes for this activity. Then gather the whole group together in the center of the room. Have the scribe from each group read that group's list. Ask:

● **What things did you miss about the other group's members?**

● **What does this activity tell us about each other?**

Say: **This activity shows us how important each person is to the whole group. We each have special qualities that make us important. When someone dies, we miss those qualities.**

4 ▸ Faith vs. fear

(Ask your senior pastor ahead of time to join you for the last half of this meeting. Explain that the meeting is about death and that kids will prepare questions to ask about death. Have your senior pastor also prepare to briefly tell how deaths in the congregation affect a pastor. For each person, you'll need a 3×5 card and a pencil.)

Give kids each a 3×5 card and a pencil. Have kids each write on their card one or more questions they have about death. Tell kids they can ask any questions they want to, but encourage them to be serious. Tell kids the question-writer won't be identified when a question is read.

Have your senior pastor talk to the kids for a few minutes about death. While the pastor is talking, shuffle through the 3×5 cards and choose no more than eight questions that are appropriate for discussion.

After the pastor finishes sharing, read aloud the questions you picked out. Have the pastor answer as many as time allows. Then thank the pastor for sharing with the class.

5 ▸ God loves us through death

(For each person, you'll need a photocopy of the "Faith and Hope" handout on page 126.)

Give kids each a "Faith and Hope" handout. Say: **As part of our closing, I'll read scripture verses that can help you deal with your feelings about death. As we read, think about how the verses can make your faith strong and give you hope.**

I'll read the teacher part and everyone else will read the people's part.

Lead kids in the responsive reading, then say: **Earlier, I quoted part of a scripture verse about death. It was from Romans 6:23 and said: "When someone sins, he earns what sin pays—death." But there's one more sentence in that verse. The verse continues: "But God gives us a free gift—life forever in Christ Jesus our Lord." Let's rejoice in that gift!**

6 Eternal-life sundaes

(You'll need ice cream, brownies, chocolate syrup, M&M's, bowls and spoons.)

End your meeting by helping kids prepare "eternal-life sundaes." Say: **Let's make sundaes to celebrate the "sweetness" of God's gift of eternal life.**

Have kids each place a brownie in their bowl; then have them top the brownie with ice cream, chocolate syrup and M&M's. Enjoy the ice cream treat with your kids as a reminder of God's gift of eternal life.

Death Fears

Instructions: Fill in a name at the top of each column. Then read through the columns and place a checkmark next to the feelings you have about each person.

Your parent's name

_____

When I think about this person dying, I feel:

☐ sad

☐ afraid

☐ alone

☐ full of questions

☐ disappointed

☐ anxious

☐ prepared

Other feelings:

_____
_____
_____
_____
_____
_____

Your best friend's name

_____

When I think about this person dying, I feel:

☐ sad

☐ afraid

☐ alone

☐ full of questions

☐ disappointed

☐ anxious

☐ prepared

Other feelings:

_____
_____
_____
_____
_____
_____

Your name

_____

When I think about this person dying, I feel:

☐ sad

☐ afraid

☐ alone

☐ full of questions

☐ disappointed

☐ anxious

☐ prepared

Other feelings:

_____
_____
_____
_____
_____
_____

Faith and Hope

Instructions: After this responsive reading, keep this handout. Refer to the verses below when you feel afraid of death or when someone you love dies.

Teacher: **The Lord is close to everyone who prays to him** (Psalm 145:18a).

People: **God, we know that you know all about us.**

Teacher: **He knows how we were made; he remembers that we are dust** (Psalm 103:14).

People: **Sometimes we're afraid because we don't know what will happen in the future.**

Teacher: **So always be ready. You don't know the day or the time the Son of Man will come** (Matthew 25:13).

People: **Sometimes we forget to share our worries with you, Lord.**

Teacher: **Come to me, all of you who are tired and have heavy loads. I will give you rest** (Matthew 11:28).

People: **We're sad when someone we love dies.**

Teacher: **But God will destroy death forever. The Lord God will wipe away every tear from every face** (Isaiah 25:8a).

People: **Thank you Lord for the greatest gift of all, the gift of eternal life.**

All: **We ask all these things in Jesus' name. Amen.**

When Parents Divorce

Y ou probably already know the bad news: Divorce touches the lives of hundreds of thousands of kids. But do you know the good news? Recent surveys indicate that the divorce rate is declining. It seems couples now have a more realistic picture of what marriage entails.

That's great news. But divorce still happens, and battle scars still exist in the lives of many elementary kids.

This meeting will help kids deal with their feelings about divorce—whether or not they come from a broken family.

Objectives

In this meeting, elementary kids will:
- understand how people touched by divorce might feel;
- discover how God feels about divorce;
- learn they're not to blame if their parents divorce; and
- thank God for helping them deal with painful things such as divorce.

The Meeting

1 People bingo

(For each person, you'll need a photocopy of the "People Bingo" handout on page 131 and a pencil. Have prizes available, such as coupons for fast-food restaurants.)

Give kids each a "People Bingo" handout and a pencil. Explain that the goal of the activity is to find people who match the descriptions in each of the bingo squares and have them sign the appropriate squares. If your group is large enough, ask that kids get a different signature in each square.

by
Margaret Hinchey

Give kids three minutes to complete the activity. Award prizes to kids who have the most signatures. Or play until someone gets all the squares filled in, and award a prize to that person.

2 Finding feelings

(You'll need two sheets of newsprint, tape, a marker and a Bible. On each sheet of newsprint, write one of the following headings: "Before the divorce" or "After the divorce." Tape the sheets of newsprint to the wall.)

Say: **You've learned some important and some not-so-important things about the kids in our group. Now we'll spend time learning about some very important things—our feelings.**

Today we're going to talk about something that's touched most of our lives. How many of you know of someone who's divorced?

Most, if not all, kids will raise their hands.

Ask kids to think about the feelings kids have just before and after their parents get a divorce. As kids call out feelings, list them on the appropriate sheet of newsprint. If kids don't know of anyone with divorced parents, have them imagine how kids might feel.

After a couple of minutes, ask:
● **What are the most common feelings we listed?**
● **Why do some couples get divorced?**

Read aloud Malachi 2:16. Say: **The Bible tells us God doesn't like divorce. But the Bible also tells us people can be forgiven for their sins. First John 1:9 says: "But if we confess our sins, he will forgive our sins. We can trust God. He does what is right. He will make us clean from all the wrongs we have done."**

3 Who's to blame?

(For each group of six or fewer, you'll need a basketball and a football—of any size. For each person, you'll need a photocopy of the "Good Words for God's People" handout on page 132 and a pencil.)

Form groups of six or fewer, and give each group a basketball. Have groups each form a circle. Say: **Bounce the basketball around your circle. Before you bounce the ball to some-**

one, call that person's name. Take turns bouncing the ball to each other.

After a couple of minutes, call time. Then give groups each a football. Have them attempt to bounce it to each other like they did with the basketball.

After a couple of minutes, ask:

● **How easy was it to bounce the basketball to someone? the football?**

● **Why is it harder to bounce a football to someone than it is to bounce a basketball?**

● **Whose fault was it that the football didn't always go where you wanted it to?**

Say: **Just like kids aren't to blame when the football bounces funny, kids aren't to blame when their parents get divorced.**

But many times, kids feel like it's their fault when their parents don't get along. Look at the feeling words on the newsprint. How do we respond to friends who have feelings like these? Sometimes it's tough to know the right words to say at the right time. The Bible can give us ideas of what to say to others—and ourselves.

Give kids each a "Good Words for God's People" handout and a pencil. Have kids each read and complete the handout. Then form groups of five or fewer and have kids discuss their completed handouts.

Ask:

● **How can these verses comfort a friend whose parents are divorced?**

● **How can these verses help you?**

4 Feeling charades

Say: **Divorce is a painful thing. But you need to tell friends and parents how you feel about painful things.**

Have kids form a circle. Ask kids to think about how they feel about divorce. Then have them each act out the feeling they're thinking about. For example, someone who feels angry might stomp his or her feet or make an angry facial expression. While kids are acting out their feelings, call freeze and have kids freeze where they are. Ask kids to look around at each other.

Ask:

● **Does everyone have the same feelings about divorce? Why or why not?**

Say: **It's okay to have different feelings about divorce. You may feel angry or upset or even relieved. But the main thing to understand is that God loves us no matter what we feel. And we need to remember children aren't to blame for parents' divorces.**

5 Closing worship

(No supplies needed.)

As a closing for this meeting, have the group join in a "popcorn" prayer. Begin the prayer by saying: **Dear God, thank you for loving us. Help us deal with painful things such as divorce. And thank you for . . .**

Say a word or phrase that describes something to be thankful for, then have kids "pop out" words or phrases as they feel comfortable doing so.

Then close by saying: **We pray these things in Jesus' name, amen.**

6 Sharing snacks

(You'll need snacks that can be shared such as two-packs of Twinkies or cookies, bunches of bananas or six-packs of soft drinks.)

Say: **Whether your parents are divorced or your friends' parents are, it's important to share how you feel with your friends. Today we're also going to share snacks with friends.**

Have kids each share their treat with at least one other person in the room. Remind kids that sharing doubles our happiness and helps lessen our sadness.

People BINGO

Instructions: The purpose of People Bingo is to learn more about our friends. Go around the room looking for people who fit the descriptions in the squares. Ask them to sign their names in the appropriate squares. The grace spaces are free—like God's love for us!

Someone who lives in the same-color house as you	Someone who has a friend with divorced parents	Someone who plays competitive sports	Someone who has a step-parent
Someone who likes to read	Someone who can recite John 3:16	Someone who has the same-color toothbrush as you	GRACE SPACE (It's free!)
Someone who got an A in math last year	GRACE SPACE (It's free!)	Someone who wears the same size shoes as you	Someone who likes broccoli
Someone who went to Sunday school last Sunday	Someone who has gone snow-skiing	Someone who has the same number of brothers and sisters as you	Someone who rides a bus to school

Good Words for God's People

Instructions: Read the situations below. Mark an X next to what you'd say to the person in each situation. Then draw a line from the story to the ''Good Words From God'' section or sections that might help the person feel better about the situation.

Good Words From God

"Do for other people what you want them to do for you."
Luke 6:31

"If my father and mother leave me, the Lord will take me in."
Psalm 27:10

"I will not leave you alone like orphans. I will come back for you."
John 14:18

"The Lord your God is a merciful God. He will not leave you or destroy you."
Deuteronomy 4:31a

"So you must stop telling lies. Tell each other the truth because we all belong to each other in the same body."
Ephesians 4:25

Situation

1. Danny comes home from school one day to find his dad has moved out. His mom tells Danny not to worry because things will probably be better without Dad around. The next day in school you notice Danny is very quiet. He tells you his story. What might help Danny?

_____ (a) It's okay, Danny. Lots of kids have divorced parents.

_____ (b) I can understand how you feel. If my dad left, I'd miss him a lot.

_____ (c) You'll probably be better off without him around. Your parents probably fought all the time anyway.

2. Jennifer is crying at her desk when you walk into your room at school. It's Friday and everyone else is happy. When you ask why she's crying, she explains that it's her weekend to stay with her dad and his new wife. She loves her dad but doesn't feel good that he's remarried. It just doesn't feel right and she dreads the weekend. What would you say?

_____ (a) Maybe you need to give your dad's wife a chance. She may be okay after all.

_____ (b) Can't you pretend you're sick or something and just get out of going?

_____ (c) Could you be honest with your dad and tell him how you feel about spending time with him and his new wife?

3. Jason was fun to be around until his parents got a divorce. Then he became quiet and didn't want to do anything with other kids. You know that he lives with his dad and that his dad works at a factory until 2 a.m. each night. What would you say?

_____ (a) Boy, I'd be scared if I had to stay alone in our house every night.

_____ (b) Jason, would you like to come over and have dinner at our house tonight? I'm sure my parents won't mind.

_____ (c) I think it's terrible that your dad is never home. You must feel like an orphan.

Serving Others

What's a servant?

Kids today may not understand servanthood. Our society preaches: "*I'm* more important than anyone else." That's light years away from servanthood. Sadly, giving of yourself to help others is a rare theme in today's movies, TV shows and songs.

But through this meeting, kids can learn what serving is all about. By seeing how they can serve one another, kids can learn how fun it is to give. And by learning how Jesus was the greatest servant of all, kids can see the importance of serving.

Objectives

In this meeting elementary kids will:
- discuss the need for service and list service activities;
- practice serving each other;
- plan a service activity to do on their own time; and
- learn how Jesus served others.

The Meeting

1 Earthquake at the banquet

(Arrange chairs in a circle. You'll need one less chair than kids.)

Have everyone except one person sit in a circle of chairs. Tell the extra person to stand in the center of the circle.

Say: **Each chair represents a table at a banquet. Each of you is a server. Some of you are serving baked ham, some are serving mashed potatoes and the rest are serving pumpkin pie.**

Assign kids each one of the items to "serve."

Say: **When the person in the center of the circle calls out what you're serving, you must get up and find a new chair to sit in. If he or she calls out "earthquake at the banquet," everyone must find a new seat.**

by
Janet Kageler

The person in the middle begins the game by calling out one of the three items being served: baked ham, mashed potatoes or pumpkin pie. Then everyone "serving" this item gets up and finds a new chair. If the person in the center of the circle calls out, "earthquake at the banquet," everyone changes chairs. Whenever people get up to move, the person in the center tries to sit in a vacated chair before anyone else can sit there. When all the chairs are full, there'll be a new person left without a chair. That person then stands in the center of the circle for the next round of the game.

Play at least eight rounds of the game.

2 How can we serve?

(You'll need a Bible, posterboard, tape and a stack of old magazines.)

Say: **The opening game was fun because we got to run around and laugh. When we think of serving others, we may think of hard work or doing things we don't want to do. But serving can also be fun.**

Ask:
- **What does it mean to serve others?**
- **Is serving others an easy thing to do? Why or why not?**

Read aloud Galatians 5:13. Ask:
- **What are ways we can serve others?**

Form groups of five or fewer. Give groups each a sheet of posterboard, some tape and a stack of old magazines. Have groups search through the magazines to find words and pictures that depict serving. Have them tear pictures and words out of the magazines and tape them to the posterboard to create a collage depicting what it means to serve others.

Have groups each show their completed collage to the rest of the groups. Have groups explain how the pictures and words depict serving.

Read aloud Matthew 20:26-28. Ask:
- **What does this passage tell us about serving others?**
- **How was Jesus a servant?**

3 Serving snacks

(You'll need assorted nuts and fruit, bowls, spoons, napkins, paper and pencils.)

Form pairs and have everyone stand. Have the partner in each pair whose birthday is closest to Christmas be the "servant" for the next activity. Say: **The servants will soon be asked to serve their partners in a number of different ways. The serving partners must follow my instructions. But during the activity, no one may speak.**

One at a time, give the following instructions to the serving partners. Be sure to allow time for each activity to be completed.

- **Give your partner a back rub.**
- **Help your partner find a comfortable seat in the room.**
- **With hand motions and facial expressions, show your partner you care for him or her.**
- **Get your partner a bowl of treats that he or she wants. Remember, you can't speak to each other. Use hand motions and gestures to figure out which treats your partner wants.**
- **Get your partner a sheet of paper and a pencil.**

Tell the servant partners to sit down. Say to the partners who were served: **Write a thank-you note to the person who served you during this activity, then give it to that person.**

Then say: **Sometimes serving others can be fun. And sometimes people are thankful for being served. But when we serve others, we don't always get something in return. Today, for example, some of you were served and some of you were servants.**

Ask:
- **How did you feel as you were served?**
- **How did you feel as you served someone else?**

Have servers and servants switch roles and follow the same serving instructions as before. Then let kids enjoy their snacks.

4 Serving coupons

(For each person, you'll need an envelope, a pencil and a photocopy of the "Serving Coupon" handout on page 136.)

Say: **We've learned what the Bible says about serving others. And we've even practiced serving others. But we can** serve people around us in many different ways. We can serve friends by helping them with schoolwork. We can serve parents by doing chores we weren't even asked to do. And we can serve God by telling others about our faith.

Give kids each an envelope, a pencil and a "Serving Coupon" handout. Have kids each read their handout and complete the coupon for someone they can serve during the coming week. Go around the room and help kids each think of something specific they can do for a friend, parent or neighbor.

Have kids form a circle and tell what they wrote on their handouts. Then have kids each tear off their coupon, place it in their envelope and write on the envelope the name of the person they'll be serving. Encourage kids each to give or mail the envelope to that person as soon as possible. Ask kids to remind each other during the week to follow through on their servant acts.

5 Serving closing

Have kids close their eyes as you read aloud Matthew 5:3-10. After each verse, pause and have everyone repeat aloud: "Lord, teach us to be servants."

Close with a short prayer, thanking God for teaching us how to serve others.

Serving Coupon

Think about what you can do to serve someone. Then write what you'll do on the coupon below. Be sure to write the person's name and describe what you'll do for that person.

Some things you might choose: do yard work for an elderly or ill church member; help a parent clean the attic or paint a room; or prepare a snack for a friend. Think up your own idea, then write it below.

- ✂ - -

To _____

I'm learning what it means to serve others as Jesus did. And to serve you, I'm going

to _____

_____.

I'm glad I'll be able to serve you in this small way.

Signed_____

Date _____Telephone number_____